SPIRITUAL GUIDES
FOR THE 21ST CENTURY

FAITH STORIES
OF THE PROTESTANT
REFORMERS

SPIRITUAL GUIDES for the 21st CENTURY

K. JAMES STEIN

UPPER
ROOM BOOKS®
NASHVILLE

The publisher gratefully acknowledges permission to reproduce the copyrighted material appearing in this book.
Credit lines for this material appear in the Permissions and Notes Section, which begins on page 224.

Cover and Interior Design: Uttley/DouPonce DesignWorks
www.uddesignworks.com

Image of Martin Luther reproduced from *Thirty-Five Years of Luther Research*
by Professor J. M. Reu. Copyright © 1917 Wartburg Publishing House.

Image of Ulrich Zwingli reproduced from *The Mountain Boy of Wildhaus: A Life of Ulric Zwingli*
by David Van Horne. Copyright © 1884 Reformed Church Publication Board.

Image of John Calvin reproduced from *The Life of John Calvin* by Thomas Lawson.
Copyright © 1884 W. Wileman.

Image of Menno Simons from *History of the Mennonite Brethren in Christ Church*
edited by Jasper Abraham Huffman. Copyright © 1920 The Bethel Publishing Company.

Cover and interior image of Thomas Cranmer from Corbis Images.

Cover image of "Martin Luther Outside All Saint's Church" from Corbis Images.

First printing: 2000
The Upper Room® Web site: http://www.upperroom.org

Library of Congress Cataloging-in-Publication Data

Stein, K. James.
    Spiritual guides for the 21st century : faith stories of the Protestant reformers / by K. James Stein.
        p. cm.
    ISBN 0-8358-0921-8
    1. Christian biography. 2. Reformers—Biography. I. Title: Spiritual guides for the
    twenty-first century. II. Title.

BR1702.S73 2000
280'.4'0922—dc21
[B]   00-020165

To Rueben P. Job,
respected bishop of the church,
faithful channel of God's grace in words spoken and printed,
cherished friend since college roommate days a half-century ago

CONTENTS

*M*any persons have assisted me in the writing of this book. Linda Koops, efficient and gracious program assistant for educational technologies at Garrett-Evangelical Theological Seminary, faithfully typed the manuscript. Janice T. Grana, executive editor of Upper Room Books, offered invaluable editorial advice throughout the writing project. Sarah Schaller-Linn of the Upper Room Books staff diligently monitored the copyright permission process. Holly Parker Halverson carefully did the final editing and formatting of the manuscript as it went to press.

Along the way three discerning readers, Ray Sluss, trusted friend, Will Jewson, and the Reverend Jane Daniels, former students, offered helpful comment upon the work-in-progress. Dr. Philip Anderson, professor of church history at North Park Theological Seminary in Chicago, read the completed manuscript for historical accuracy.

I gratefully acknowledge the time and energy these people gave in helping bring this work to completion. It goes without saying that should errors in fact or interpretation still linger in the text, they are mine and not theirs.

In the thirty-six years of teaching church history at Garrett-Evangelical Theological Seminary, I have been privileged to teach hundreds of students who have heard the lectures and read the primary sources from which much of this text has been drawn. It was a joy to share with them the colorful history and grace-filled theology that was the essence of the Protestant Reformation. These students inspired and challenged me, and to them I pay grateful tribute.

*J*oshua 4 records a significant event in the history of salvation. As the Hebrew people were crossing the Jordan River, Joshua ordered twelve men, one from each tribe, to pick up a stone from the now-dry riverbed where the priests stood bearing the ark of the covenant. From these stones they were to build a memorial, Joshua explained, "so that this may be a sign among you. When your children ask in time to come, 'What do those stones mean to you?' then you shall tell them that the waters of the Jordan were cut off in front of the ark of the covenant of the Lord. When it crossed over the Jordan, the waters of the Jordan were cut off. So these stones shall be to the Israelites a memorial forever" (Josh. 4:6–8).

This story recounts something essentially human. Long before and after this occurrence, people have built memorials, painted pictures, composed music, and authored documents and books so that significant events would not fade from common memory. The Judeo-Christian heritage stands upon the cardinal belief that God has acted and acts in human history to provide salvation and to call forth a people whose unique mission has been to share this with the rest of the human race. The great festivals and weekly services of worship in both Judaism and Christianity are premised upon this basic faith commitment. Christianity's three major branches—Eastern Orthodoxy, Roman Catholicism, and Protestantism—stress particular meanings that emerge from the past. As Christians live in the present and face an uncertain future, historical events inform, inspire, and shape their lives.

To be sure, many contemporary Protestants belong to denominations that emerged as late as the nineteenth or twentieth centuries.

Such persons, however, must admit that in addition to claiming the church's history in the patristic age (the first five centuries) and the medieval period, they are also directly or indirectly affected by the stirring events in sixteenth-century Europe that their ancestors have labeled the Protestant Reformation.

Even though the Reformation happened nearly five centuries ago, its story still makes interesting reading. It recalls the head-on struggle between conflicting theologies, the determined actions of outstanding leaders, and the unjust treatment of innocent people on both sides. Theology alone did not drive these complicated events; political, economic, national, military, and social considerations, similar to those we see in religious struggles in our own times, also played significant roles. Primarily a religious movement, the Protestant Reformation was and is instructive for us yet today. The issues that Protestants and their Roman Catholic counterparts struggled over then still shape the manner in which their descendants believe and live their Christian lives half a millennium later.

In order to cope with the unknown challenges of the twenty-first century, Christians will need a stout faith, grounded in their knowledge of God's self-revelation in Jesus Christ. The primary source that the Holy Spirit will use to arouse such confidence will continue to be the holy scriptures. A secondary fountain of knowledge and inspiration from which contemporary Protestant Christians may draw is the testimony left by their reforming forebears of the sixteenth century. Rich resources for faith and life are there in Martin Luther's understanding of how we can become free people in Christ, in Ulrich Zwingli's confidence in the power contained in God's word, in John Calvin's belief that to be a Christian is to be owned by the God to whose glory one daily and gratefully lives, in Menno Simons's contention that the New Birth results in highly committed disciples, and in Thomas Cranmer's essential reminder that this theology is best lived out when prayed with articulate and penetrating language. To suggest that the Reformers offer guidance to fellow Christians living five centuries later is to make no empty claim. It is to say that their basic message of Christian faith can stir us up to vital discipleship in our own time. This is a healthy use of "the communion of saints" most Christians acknowledge when they affirm the Apostles' Creed.

Although this book seeks to be a memorial to the Protestant Reformation, I must offer certain disclaimers concerning its style and content. For one thing, it is not a scholar's book. Although it relies on sound research, it is more a popular version of the story of the Reformation. I have written it especially for interested laypersons who may occasionally ask why Protestants believe certain doctrines and not others, engage in some worship practices and not others, or are not bound to the same disciplinary requirements that offer meaning to their Roman Catholic brothers and sisters in Christ.

Second, it is not an anti-Catholic book. It happily acknowledges that Protestants and Roman Catholics are increasingly finding common ground and unity of purpose in many areas in the early twenty-first century. Therefore it portrays the Protestant Reformation, to use Jaroslav Pelikan's term, as a "tragic necessity"[1]; it reviews the sixteenth-century battles as a "family fight." Although I am appreciative of my lifelong Protestant nurture, I want this book also to reflect my appreciation for the Roman Catholic church. Dismissing from the beginning any idealistic (and unattainable) claim to objective reporting of the facts, I seek to offer a fair and evenhanded account of the persons and events central to this story.

Third, it is not a unique book. A vast amount of material regarding the Protestant Reformation is already in print. Please view this history instead as my attempt to share more widely my own learnings and insights drawn together during thirty-six years as a professor of church history. This subject has become, for me, the most exciting segment of the colorful, dramatic, and often sad account of the church's two-thousand-year existence. I present it with the fervent hope that you will discover new ways of being grounded in God's salvation through Jesus Christ and, thus fortified in your faith, you will be all the more fruitful in the ministry, lay or clerical, to which God has called you in the world.

Finally, this book depends upon the work of other people. The insights I share in these pages could not appear without the scholarly labors of men and women whose publications I gratefully acknowledge. One book deserving special mention is Robert McAfee Brown's *The Spirit of Protestantism.* Although now in some ways outdated, it still proves a valuable resource for contemporary students of the Reformation. Brown contends that the Reformation was never finished, that reformation needs to continue in the life of the church, and that the spirit of Protestantism is "an openness to the judging and renewing activity of the living God made known in Jesus Christ."[2] Such a contention summons you, the present reader of an account of the sixteenth-century Reformation, to ask where and how God through the Holy Spirit is reforming you and the church in the current day.

Herein, then, we come to study the "stones" that previous scholars and believers gathered from their own Jordan experiences. As we ponder God's maneuvering in the lives of the Protestant reformers, may we take the opportunity to celebrate and remember God's enlivening work in our own.

The World into Which the Reformation Came

The Jorvik Viking Centre is an interesting museum in York, England. The name *Jorvik* is the Viking designation for the town in northeastern England that the Vikings captured and resettled in 867. The unique thing about the Jorvik is that as soon as sight-seers board its little "time cars," they are transported into the past. They pass one diorama after another, each representing earlier states of the city's history through the use of life-sized human figures that portray the dress, housing, utensils, and weapons of the time period. Visitors to the Jorvik Viking Centre receive an understanding of York's history as they work their way backward into it.

So it is with the Protestant Reformation. To understand it, we must work our way backward into it. By doing so we quickly discern that it was not a purely religious phenomenon. A combination of political, social, and economic factors interlaced with Renaissance intellectual and cultural concerns to set the stage upon which the Reformation could happen. A brief backward glance into the world of the sixteenth-century western Europe will help us know the territory in which this dynamic movement occurred.

THE POLITICAL BACKGROUND
OF SIXTEENTH-CENTURY EUROPE

In many ways the Reformation can be viewed as a struggle between a growing nationalism in various European countries and an international church headed by the papacy. One detects this in the northern European nations which sought independence from the pope and hierarchy in Rome. A brief review, therefore, of the major political powers of sixteenth-century Europe is needed.

Spain, with a population of about eight million people, was about the size it is today. King Ferdinand and Queen Isabella affirmed their royal power against the nobility and the common people. One threat to Spanish unity was the presence of sizeable Jewish and Moslem minorities. For many years tolerance reigned, but then religious hatred flared. As a result, the Spanish Inquisition sentenced two thousand people to be burned as heretics and one hundred thousand to be exiled. A fanatical devotion to Roman Catholic Christianity, far surpassing that of other European nations, could then thrive unabated.

With sixteen million people, France also was seeking to consolidate its power. King Francis I made France an ally of the popes. This led to intermittent war between Spain and France throughout the Reformation era. France felt surrounded by Spain and the Holy Roman Empire. Yet historians have deemed France the most self-sufficient country of its time, contending that "nowhere else in Europe was there such a large and relatively homogeneous people under a single government which could make its will felt in all corners of the land."[1]

England's population at the beginning of the sixteenth century was roughly four million. The British crown, while wealthy, still felt limitations on its power. For example, the king's authority depended not on a standing army but on popular approval. The royal power ruled the nation, but Parliament controlled its purse strings. As the century progressed, Parliament grew in influence.

Italy, like Germany, would have to wait until the nineteenth century for political unity. In the sixteenth century, Italy was divided into three major parts. Northern Italy was considered the cultural center of sixteenth-century Europe. The many city-states of northern Italy were really dictatorships. The petty monarchs who ruled them maintained their powers by using mercenary soldiers. Each city-state included the countryside surrounding the fortified towns. Manufacturing and commerce provided the economic support of these city-states.

The papal states, always afraid of encirclement, often connived against their northern and southern neighbors. The papal states had the unenviable reputation of being the worst-administered territory in Europe, being lawless, often bankrupt and corrupt. The popes, as leaders of civil government, remained entangled in the political and military struggles of the times.

For two hundred years, southern Italy, as well as Sicily and Sardinia, had belonged to Spain. France, desiring to control this part of Italy, triggered several European wars.

The Turkish Ottoman Empire was expanding its borders in the sixteenth century. Its conquest of Hungary in 1526 and unsuccessful siege of Vienna in 1529 made the Turks a constant threat to western Christendom during this time. As a threat to the Holy Roman Empire from the east, they often inadvertently gave political and military breathing space to the insurgent Lutheran princes.

The Holy Roman Empire, stretching from the Adriatic Sea in the south to the Baltic Sea in the north and from the Oder River on the east westward across the Rhine, had a population of about twenty million people. Predominantly German, it was a loose-knit confederation of variously sized states and fifty-one free cities. The emperor presided over it with only nominal authority. There was no standing army, regular taxation system, or unified judiciary. War between states of the empire was frequent.

Since the fourteenth century new emperors had been chosen by seven designated electors. Three of these were church leaders: the archbishops of Mainz, Trier, and Cologne. The other four electors were secular rulers: the Margrave of Brandenburg, the King of Bohemia, the Elector of the Palatinate, and the Elector of Saxony. This situation would have telling effect in the Lutheran Reformation.

Political issues within the Roman Catholic church greatly influenced sixteenth-century Europe. In the Middle Ages the Roman Catholic church suffered temporary division. Between 1309 and 1377 there were two competitive popes—one in Rome and another in Avignon in southern France. A council held at Pisa, Italy, in 1409 to resolve this unfortunate situation only worsened matters. As a result, three popes attempted to govern the church between 1409 and 1417—each condemning the others and contending for the loyalties of the European nations.

Resolution of this problem came in the early fifteenth century. The Council of Constance, a gathering of bishops and theologians, forced the resignation of the three existing popes and elected a new one. This ushered in what became known as "the conciliar movement," wherein bishops meeting in council asserted their powers against the papacy in Rome.

This was aggravated by the fact that for several centuries some bishops had functioned simultaneously as civil and spiritual leaders. They collected taxes, built roads, and led armies as temporal rulers and dedicated church buildings, presided at synod meetings, and ordained clergy as spiritual rulers. These bishops, in effect, controlled large geographic areas and exercised great political power.

In the fifteenth and early sixteenth centuries the papacy entered into agreements with the rising nation-states of Europe to curtail the power of its own bishops. This introduced the idea of the territorial church—one whose real head was the civil government—which would have far-reaching consequences for the Reformation.

Another major political issue in Europe was the choice of the Holy Roman Emperor. Even before the Holy Roman Emperor (Maximilian I) died in 1519, the political talk of Europe concerned the choice of his successor. The ailing emperor clearly preferred his grandson, King Charles I of Spain. King Francis I of France wanted the job for himself. Pope Leo X (1513–21), hesitant to support either Spain or France (the superpowers of the time), favored Frederick the Wise, the Elector of Saxony. Frederick, while not too powerful, had a proven reputation as a reliable politician. The papacy's courtship of Frederick the Wise included the suggestion that a cardinal's hat could be bestowed on one of his ordained subjects. It may have been an attempt to silence the already troublesome Luther![2] Frederick was not persuaded, however, to seek the office of emperor or to confer special privileges upon Luther.[3]

In June 1519 the seven electors unanimously chose King Charles of Spain as the new emperor. The slender nineteen-year-old was now not only the ruler of Spain but Emperor Charles V. A devout Roman Catholic, he opposed the Protestant Reformation. He would become so busy, however, putting down a rebellion in Spain, fighting a Franco-papal alliance, and facing the Turks in the east that he lacked the time and resources to crush the Lutheran revolt. His nine-year absence from the German-speaking portion of his empire allowed Lutheranism to gain a strong foothold.

THE SOCIOECONOMIC BACKGROUND

Capitalism, using money to make money, emerged as an economic reality at the close of the fifteenth and the beginning of the sixteenth centuries. Evidence of the changing economic picture lay in the appearance of international money markets at Antwerp, Lyon, and Genoa; in the printing press as the first mechanized industry to use the principle of interchangeable parts and to turn out a standardized product; and in the use of strikes by urban workers at Lyon in 1539.[4] International banking with double-entry bookkeeping, checks, and drafts was developing. Trade inside and outside Europe enhanced this mercantile and financial activity. Europe's towns began to prosper. The craft guilds rose to prominence alongside the wealthy merchant class. Until this time the nobility, the clergy, and the peasants had formed the three social classes. Now the townspeople, the bourgeoisie, emerged as a fourth social class.

Unemployment began to be a problem at the end of the fifteenth century, due in part to the inflation caused by the importing of tons of gold and silver from America and by the reduction of business and commerce to prevent the export of money through trade. Wars, epidemics, and unregulated commerce also caused unemployment.

The unemployed migrated from place to place, looking for work. Their presence alongside the poor and those with handicapping conditions caused the towns increasingly to take over "poor legislation" from the church. Almsgiving had played a significant role in medieval piety, but little was done to solve the problems of the unfortunate. In the sixteenth century the towns created public-works programs to help the migrant "sturdy poor" until they could get on their feet. Begging was increasingly looked upon with disfavor.

Little wonder that when the Reformation came, it would receive a ready hearing in many German towns. By the seventeenth century, of the fifty-one German free cities, thirteen were Roman Catholic, thirty-four were Protestant, and four were mixed in basic religious orientation.[5] Protestantism's insistence on the potential for "works righteousness" in almsgiving, on the evil of begging, and on God's glorification by hard work in the vocations to which God called people all contributed to creating the "Protestant work ethic." In urban areas where trade and manufacture depended on people's believing in the virtues of work, such teaching found acceptance.

Some knights and barons, however, had difficulty adapting to a money economy. Like their forebears, they sought to live off their self-sufficient domains using the barter system. Now, to obtain cash for desired luxuries, they foolishly mortgaged or sold their properties. Threatened with bankruptcy, they laid heavier exactions on the peasants working their lands. Some impoverished knights took to plundering merchant wagon trains, thus becoming known as the "robber barons."

At the bottom of the medieval socioeconomic pecking order were the peasants, whose lot was particularly difficult. Bound to the land on which they lived, they sometimes needed approval to marry from the lord of the manor for whom they worked. Their lives might have been bearable had they seen any opportunity for their children and grandchildren to escape their hard lot in life. H. F. M. Prescott aptly described the peasant life: "Between long hours of labor, and nights spent on straw with a good round log for a pillow; under the shadow of death and, worse still, of sickness unrelieved by anything but the crudest medical science; in great discomfort and many fears; in the midst of beauty untouched by any ugliness save that of dirt, disease, or death, the common people passed their lives."[6]

The continual snubbing peasants faced from the nobility and the rising middle class added to the harsh conditions of their existence. Considered the laughingstock of society, the peasants naturally turned a ready ear to any movement offering the prospect of a better future.

THE CHURCH IN SIXTEENTH-CENTURY EUROPE

Four major emphases characterized church life during this period. The first of these was the belief that the church's seven sacraments conferred grace, the divine unmerited favor. Baptism washed away people's guilt of original sin and sealed them into Christ. Confirmation granted persons the Holy Spirit and enrolled them as soldiers of Christ. The Eucharist offered the body and blood of Christ, who in the mass was sacrificed afresh on the altar. In marriage, husband and wife conveyed grace to each other that promised to bind them in an indissoluble union broken only by death. Penance delivered grace for the forgiveness of sin and the remission of its punishments. Ordination set men aside to Christ's sacramental ministry, according them the unequaled power to offer the body and blood of Christ. Extreme unction provided grace for the dying as they departed this life and began their journey to God. Underlying all these sacraments lay the belief that God used natural objects as well as words to bestow grace on those with faith to receive it.

The Lord's Supper or Eucharist, the central and most frequently administered sacrament, was offered at each Sunday mass. Since 1215 Roman Catholics were expected to receive the Eucharist as well as appear at confession at least once a year. Roman Catholic theology taught that by the action of the Holy Spirit, when the priest elevated the bread and wine, these elements became the body and blood of Christ.

The word used traditionally to describe what happened at mass was *transubstantiation*, which meant that the substance (inner reality) was changed from bread to body and from wine to blood, even though the accidents (outward characteristics) remained the same. Even though fewer persons today use the term *transubstantiation*, Roman Catholics still believe that in the mass they actually receive Christ's body and blood.

Interestingly, taking Communion at mass was considered a beneficial good work for laypersons as much as it was for priests, who said mass daily. Moreover, a multiplication of masses said on one's behalf after death would "add stars to one's crown." Rich and powerful persons provided funds in their wills to procure the saying of many masses for their souls after they died.

A second emphasis of medieval church life included making pilgrimages and venerating relics. This practice began in the early church when our Lord's disciples began to venerate places made meaningful by events in his life and places where imperial Rome's persecution created many martyrs. Early Christians gathered the bones and possessions of those who died for the faith and soon required that the relics of saints and martyrs be placed under the altars of new church buildings.

By the Middle Ages people sought spiritual benefits by praying before the relics of Christian heroes and martyrs. The favorite pilgrimage site in western Europe was Rome, but each nation had its own relic collection to accommodate those who could not make the arduous and expensive pilgrimage to the Eternal City.

A third aspect of medieval church life was religious drama. Modern drama, like so many significant features of our life today, arose in the church. Wandering players portrayed religious messages. Miracle and morality plays were in vogue. These dramatic presentations moved from town to town.

The Reformation occurred at a time in which compulsory popular education was unknown. The peasants were largely unlettered. Children of the nobility and the growing middle class often received a basic education from tutors (usually priests) hired by their parents. With the majority of Europe's populace still illiterate, religious drama had particular appeal. People needed no education to understand its message. Like the churches and cathedrals with their statuary and artwork, which provided the uneducated populace with the "gospel in stone" and the "gospel in stained glass," religious drama helped teach the people.

The veneration of saints was a fourth facet of popular religion. The invocation of saints in prayer had begun in the ancient church. However, as the great theologians in the universities through their philosophical theology made God and even Christ appear more remote and inaccessible to ordinary believers, the latter turned increasingly to the saints—especially to the Virgin Mary—to intercede for them. The humanity of the saints provided a warmth otherwise missing in the relationship of ordinary medieval people with God. Believers came to invoke the aid of the saints in all kinds of circumstances. To some saints they attributed powers deemed helpful in meeting particular needs: Saint Clarus of Albi supposedly helped in case of eye trouble; Saint Dennis relieved toothache; and the fourteen Helpers in Need included saints who could guard against sudden death by lightning, throat trouble, fever, tuberculosis, and epilepsy.[7]

Connected with this veneration of saints was the mounting adoration of Roman Catholics to the Virgin Mary. People prayed to her to intercede for them with Christ, for who could more effectively appeal to her son than his mother?

In looking at church life, it is important to recognize that a disagreement over the sacrament of penance actually touched off the

Protestant Reformation. The sacrament of penance, emerging from early church practice, taught that Christians with grave moral lapses would have to provide restitution for sin. Christ's atonement for sin on the cross guaranteed forgiveness, but penitents needed to make satisfaction on their own for the sins they had committed. In the early centuries the clergy excluded from Christian fellowship those guilty of serious sins and readmitted them only after they had made a convincing penitential statement before the local congregation, which would determine what kind of satisfaction might be necessary. Later, penitents needed to appear only before their priests for this purpose. By the seventh century, church policy had standardized the satisfactions that penitents had to make.

Already in the Middle Ages the sacrament of penance consisted of four parts: contrition of the heart, confession of the mouth, absolution by the priest, and satisfaction of the work. Although the priest in God's name bestowed forgiveness on penitents, the latter were required to make satisfaction by suffering a temporal punishment for sin such as fasting, restraint from sexual intercourse, pilgrimages, floggings, or imprisonment. Priests naturally sought to "make the punishment fit the crime."

Satisfaction often interrupted the ordinary flow of life. Therefore, a computation system emerged in which, instead of extending satisfaction over a long period of time or assigning an expensive pilgrimage, the church could indulge one by compressing the necessary recompense into a single penitential act like sustained repetition of psalm verses in a position of physical discomfort or making a money payment. Indulgences have been defined as "the remission granted by the church of the temporal punishment due to sins already forgiven."[8]

For example, during the Crusades, the church promised a full indulgence to anyone who would volunteer to fight the Turks. Later, indulgences were granted in return for money payments. They attained greater significance in 1476 when Pope Sixtus IV extended them to the dead in purgatory. Now relatives and friends on earth could purchase indulgence letters to reduce the temporal punishment of their loved ones in purgatory—thus enabling the latter to enter heavenly rest all the sooner.

Pope Julius II desired to celebrate the magnificence of the Roman Catholic church by erecting a basilica more glorious than ever. In 1506, he laid the foundation of the present Saint Peter's Cathedral in Rome. The sale of indulgences helped defray building costs. The mentality of the people of western Europe was such that they readily responded to indulgence salesmen.

CULTURAL CHANGES IN THE SIXTEENTH CENTURY

The Middle Ages have been known as the "Age of Faith." Emphasizing the otherworldly, their orientation toward the spiritual side of life is most obvious in their sense of grandeur that even the misery of disease, poverty, brevity of life, and political chaos could not negate. Because medieval people believed, they built. The great cathedrals soaring upward to God and the papacy's attempts to rule both church and state exemplify human aspiration focused on God.

The Renaissance was a reaction to this. It occurred roughly between 1300 and the early or mid-sixteenth century.[9] It was basically a rebirth or a reemphasis of life as it had been lived in Greco-Roman times before medieval otherworldliness appeared.

The Renaissance did not usher in a rebirth of learning. Learning had continued throughout the turbulent Dark Ages (between A.D. 400 and 800), when the barbaric invasions were dismantling the

Roman Empire. Rather, the Renaissance has been aptly described as a rebirth "of mind and soul which was manifesting itself in literature, art, theology, education, science, political thought, exploration, and invention."[10]

There were two dominating aspects to the Renaissance. The first, humanism, technically was a literary movement—a revival of interest in ancient authors and their works. The spirit of antiquity could be recaptured by making use of the literature of that period.

As a research and learning method, humanism effected significant changes in western Europe. It quickened the intellect and enhanced scientific discovery. It aroused a greater sense of history. Its concern to authenticate ancient sources carried over into biblical studies and church history. Its study of antiquity's documents uncovered a spirit of freedom and the right of private judgment that emboldened literary critics who remained within the medieval church, as well as those who became Protestant reformers.

Although somewhat similar, the Renaissance and the Reformation were not the same. Humanism may have stimulated the reformers to return to the scriptures as their primary authority, but here the two movements parted. The humanists prized the scriptures as ancient literary sources, but the reformers believed they heard God speaking to them from the pages of scripture. In addition, humanist authors accented human potential while the Protestant reformers took a dimmer view of human ability to get right with God.

The greatest of all humanists was Desiderius Erasmus (1466–1536), the illegitimate son of a Dutch priest and his common-law wife. Educated along with his older brother in monastic schools, Erasmus was ordained in 1492 and studied at Paris University. Invited to England, he became a close friend of the leading Christian humanists in that country, John Colet and Thomas More. While a guest in More's home, Erasmus published his *Praise of Folly* in 1509. He praised folly, which included impulse and emotion as well as ignorance and absurdity. The human race owed its existence to folly, he believed, and he courageously wrote satire about priests, monks, bishops, theologians, and popes.

Erasmus was no mere satirist, however. He loved the church and believed that it could be reformed if people would accept the enlightenment made available to all. If taught to do right, people would do so if they followed "the simple philosophy of Christ." The widely published Erasmus hoped the church could be reformed from within, without turmoil (he was a mediator) and without excessive dogma (he was a moralist, not a theologian). His patron saint was the thief on the cross who was admitted to paradise with little or no theology![11]

The other aspect of the Renaissance was its expansive mood. The accent on scholarship and human values served to push back boundaries and to bring new worlds into view. Geographic expansion occurred as Diaz in 1488 discovered the Cape of Good Hope at the southern tip of Africa; as Columbus discovered the Western Hemisphere in 1492; and as Vasco da Gama in 1498 first sailed around Africa to India, reducing the expense of trade with the east by 75 percent. Ferdinand Magellan led an expedition in 1519–22 that first circumnavigated the globe. These discoveries enhanced European knowledge and commerce.

Scientific expansion also marked the Renaissance. The Polish astronomer Nicholas Copernicus proved that we live in a heliocentric universe, although the church rejected his findings. Vesalius, a brilliant Flemish surgeon and teacher, in 1543 published *The Fabric of the Human Body*, the first work on human anatomy since the time of the ancient Greeks based on careful firsthand observation and dissection.[12]

Technological advance during the Renaissance peaked in the

invention of the printing press. This "high-tech" development parallels the importance of the computer in our time. Credit for this invention is usually accorded John Gutenberg (1395?–1468), whose press is thought to have first appeared in Mainz, Germany, in 1454. It is estimated that by 1500 more than two hundred European cities had printing presses.[13] The printing press revolutionized European life. It greatly reduced the cost of producing manuscripts; it eliminated the universities' monopoly over learning; it put the Bible into the hands of laypeople and thus reduced papal authority; it encouraged the use of vernacular languages.[14]

It is difficult to conceive of the success of the Reformation without taking the printing press into consideration. Both Protestants and Roman Catholics communicated their ideas effectively with the printed word. No one made more productive use of it than Martin Luther.

Cultural expansion also typified the Renaissance. Although nine out of ten Europeans still made their living from agriculture or related industries, urban growth and accompanying material gain created a desire for certain refinements and cultural advantages. Polyphonic music (many sounds harmonized together) originated in Italy, and opera was also born in the sixteenth century.

Architecture and the arts clearly evidenced the Renaissance focus on human aspiration. For about three centuries Gothic architecture with its square towers, high arches, and vaulted ceilings that pointed worshipers upward to God predominated in Europe. Renaissance architecture adapted ancient Greek and Roman building styles to fit fifteenth- and sixteenth-century needs. Domed roofs, columned porticoes, and facades reminiscent of ancient Greece characterized this period's structures.

Sculpture in the Middle Ages had been a decorative art, but with the Renaissance concern to recapture the human figure, sculpture came into its own. Sculptors now studied anatomy and dissection to lend realism to their work. Renaissance painters also studied human anatomy carefully. They discovered how to depict spatial relationships on flat surfaces and became adept at painting shadows and blurring their objects into the surrounding landscapes. They revealed their strong Renaissance commitment to humanity and its values, despite their focus upon biblical and religious themes.

REFORM MOVEMENTS IN THE CHURCH

The Protestant Reformation was not the first or last stride toward church renewal. A number of significant movements in the church's history emerged from time to time with positive change in mind. Several of these deserve brief mention.

In the twelfth century Peter Waldo, a wealthy Lyon merchant, felt compelled by the gospel to give away his wealth and organize the preaching of evangelical poverty by laypersons. His associates, often called "the poor men of Lyon," attracted hundreds of followers in the mountains of southern France and northern Italy. These people preferred the simple biblical preaching of the Waldensians to the pomp and social insensitivity of the medieval hierarchy. The Waldensians translated the Bible into the language of the people. Declared heretics by Rome, the Waldensians suffered terrible persecution but endured in Europe's Alpine regions. They exist as a church today and in the late twentieth century united with the Methodist Church in Italy.

The thirteenth century saw the rise of the begging orders, the Franciscans and Dominicans. The former resulted from the conversion experience of Francis of Assisi, which turned this pleasure-loving son of wealthy parents to the needs of the poor and lepers. Given papal approval, Francis organized his *fratres minores* ("little brothers"), sending them out in pairs to minister to the lowest elements in Italian society. Thousands joined his Salvation Army-type movement. A women's order, named after Clare of Assisi, aided in the mission. Francis urged joy and gladness on his followers, who called themselves "God's Jesters."

The Dominican order emerged from the labors of Dominic de Guzman, the son of a Spanish noble family. Unlike Francis, Dominic was university educated and ordained. He became convinced that the church's inefficacy in winning heretics back to the fold stemmed from its lack of knowledgeable and disciplined preachers. In 1220 the pope sanctioned his Order of Preachers. The well-educated Dominicans eventually became an arm of the Roman church's much-feared Inquisition.

In the fourteenth century a different kind of reform arose. Its leaders, John Wyclif and John Hus, have been referred to as "pre-reformers." Wyclif received his doctoral degree in theology in 1372 at Oxford University in his native England. He taught at Oxford another ten years before his criticisms of church corruption, and the support he gave to an English translation of the Bible for the common people, led Rome to force him out of his teaching position. Protected by the son of King Edward III, Wyclif retired to his Lutterworth parish, where he died. While still at Oxford he had been sending out his "poor priests" in pairs to preach to the people. They became known as Lollards. Despite intense persecution they convinced many people.

John Hus, product of a poor Bohemian family, received his master's degree from Prague University in 1396. Ordained a priest, he began a vital preaching ministry in Prague's Bethlehem Chapel in 1401. His fiery sermons, which criticized the corruption and superstitions he found in the medieval church, drew three thousand people to hear him several times a day! Hus probably was influenced by

Wyclif through the Bohemian students who brought the latter's writings home from their studies at Oxford. Hus disagreed with Wyclif's denial of the doctrine of transubstantiation.

Nationalism, which had supported Wyclif in England, played also in Hus's favor in Bohemia. Hus was excommunicated and exiled in 1410. He used this opportunity to publish his ideas. Summoned to the Council of Constance to present his views and guaranteed safe conduct, Hus went. Jailed immediately upon arrival as a heretic and tried, Hus refused to recant. He was burned at the stake on July 6, 1415. The Council of Constance also condemned Wyclif's teachings, ordered his books burned, and commanded the exhuming and burning of his body.

With the news of Hus's death, Bohemia flared into open revolt against Rome. The Hussites were finally defeated in 1434. Twenty-three years later they organized themselves into the *Unitas Fratrum* ("Unity of the Brethren"), which in small numbers survived much persecution and in the eighteenth century emigrated to Saxony where they became known as the Moravians.

A still different reform effort appeared in Florence during the last decade of the fifteenth century. It was the work of Girolamo Savonarola, an ascetic Dominican monk who attracted much attention at San Marco's church with his apocalyptic predictions of future suffering because of the sins of church and society. Believing in visions and feeling divinely led to reform the church, Savonarola attacked her abuses. However, his excommunication and the coming of plague and famine to Florence eroded Savonarola's power base. Under torture he admitted that he had received no direct communication from God as his sermons claimed. Convicted of heresy, Savonarola and two companions were hanged and burned in 1498.

The reforms that preceded Protestantism largely attempted to cleanse the church of its abuses. Although they pitted biblical authority against papal teachings, men like Wyclif and Hus saw the Bible as God's law to be obeyed. By this means they sought to call the body of Christ back to its true self.

Something new and more practical emerged in the sixteenth century. Martin Luther summed it up by saying that others had attacked the church's life, but he had attacked its doctrine.[15] He realized that it was not enough to call people to a higher level of commitment to Christ and to more consistent ethical practice. One had, on the basis of scripture, to recover the heart of the gospel in order to believe. What people really believed far outdistanced their resolution to clean up their personal or institutional lives. Consequently, he and others launched a more shattering change than the Roman Catholic church had before experienced.

In the city of Worms, Germany, stands the famous monument to Martin Luther. Placed there in an open park in 1868, it is impressive because of its size and the elaborate foundation on which it stands. At its four corners are life-sized statues of Philip Melanchthon, a Greek scholar, and his grand uncle, Johann Reuchlin, the great Hebrew scholar, along with Prince Frederick the Wise and Prince Philip of Hesse. The sculptor used these four figures to indicate that biblical scholarship and political power made Luther's Reformation possible.

The statue conveys yet another meaning. The Luther statue depicts the reformer looking straight ahead with an open Bible in his outstretched hand, towering above all else. At its base, however, in seated position, are the life-sized figures of Peter Waldo, John Wyclif, John Hus, and Girolamo Savonarola—four pre-reformers. The artist's intention is clear. Powerful and world changing as Luther's Reformation was, one must not forget that he stood on the shoulders of others.

FOR PERSONAL OR GROUP REFLECTION

1. When and under what circumstances did you became significantly aware of the Protestant Reformation? What have you heard about it?

2. How do most Protestants you know view the Reformation? as something unfinished and to be continued in our own time?

3. What areas of church life would you like to see reformed today?

4. Does the church seem less political in our modern democracy than in sixteenth-century Europe?

5. Think about the aspects you most value about your faith and church experience. Compare this with the experiences of persons in the sixteenth century. What learnings do you have?

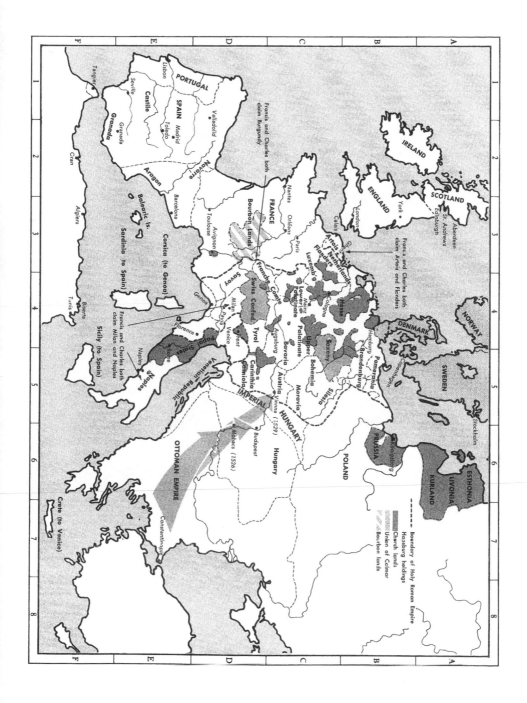

c.1454	Invention of the printing press
1483	Birth of Martin Luther
1484	Birth of Ulrich Zwingli
1489	Birth of Thomas Cranmer
1494	Birth of William Tyndale
1496	Birth of Menno Simons
1504	Birth of Heinrich Bullinger
1509	Birth of John Calvin; Henry VIII becomes King of England
1517	Luther's Ninety-five Theses
1519	Charles I of Spain becomes Holy Roman Emperor
1520	Luther's Three Great Treatises
1521	Luther's appearance at the Diet of Worms
1522–25	Zwingli's Zurich Reforms
1524–25	The Peasants' War
1525	The Anabaptist "Swiss Brethren" break with Zwingli
1529	The word *Protestant* emerges at the Diet of Speyer; Luther and Zwingli disagree on the Lord's Supper at the Marburg Colloquy
1530	The Lutherans present their Augsburg Confession
1531	Zwingli dies on the Kappel battlefield
1532–34	Henry VIII breaks England away from Rome
1533	Thomas Cranmer becomes Archbishop of Canterbury
1534–35	The Münster Tragedy

1536	First edition of John Calvin's *Institutes;* Menno Simons's conversion to Anabaptist Protestantism; execution of William Tyndale
1536–38	John Calvin's first Geneva ministry
1538–41	Calvin's Strassburg ministry
1541–64	Calvin's second Geneva ministry
1545–63	Roman Catholic Council of Trent
1546	Death of Martin Luther
1547	Death of King Henry VIII
1549/52	*Book of Common Prayer* (Church of England)
1555	Peace of Augsburg
1556	Death of Thomas Cranmer
1559	"Elizabethan Settlement" in the Church of England
1561	Death of Menno Simons
1564	Death of John Calvin
1572	Death of Heinrich Bullinger

MARTIN
LUTHER

"I Am Bound by the Scriptures"

THE LIFE AND MINISTRY OF MARTIN LUTHER

*M*artin Luther is one of the pivotal figures in both church and world history. He initiated the greatest reform movement the Western church has seen until the twentieth century. His collected works fill one hundred volumes of about seven hundred pages each, and a vast amount of books and articles have been written about him. More than just prolific, Luther was profound. His outspoken ways, earthy language, and startlingly fresh theological insights made him a powerful and charismatic leader from whom we can glean much for twenty-first-century living.

THE LIFE STORY OF MARTIN LUTHER

Luther was born on November 10, 1483, to Hans and Margaret Lindemann Luther in Eisleben, Saxony. His parents were of Saxon peasant stock—pious, strict, hardworking, and loyal to the church. The day after Luther's birth, which was Saint Martin's day, his parents had him baptized and named him after the saint. About a year later, the family moved to nearby Mansfeld so Hans could work in the growing copper industry.[1] By his becoming part owner of a prosperous mine and a town alderman, Hans Luther provided his family some upward social mobility.

Thus, unlike most of his peers, Luther was able to acquire some education. He completed studies at the local grammar school, where all instruction was in Latin. Luther must have excelled there because in 1498 he entered the Latin school at Eisenach.

Hans Luther's ambition for his obviously gifted son reflects itself in his choice of Eisenach, a good school with excellent teachers who would prepare Luther for further studies. There Luther formed life-long friendships with members of the faculty. He also "sang for his supper," as did all German students at that time, rich or poor. His pleasant manner and fine tenor voice gained him entrée to the homes of two leading Eisenach families, the Cottas and the Schalbes. A port of intellectual growth and personal nurture, Eisenach remained for Luther his "beloved town."[2]

University Years

In 1501, Luther entered Erfurt University which, with its two thousand students, was then the largest and most progressive German university. Its curriculum included the *trivium* (Latin, rhetoric, and dialectic) and the *quadrivium* (arithmetic, geometry, astronomy, and music). The faculty emphasized academic disputations in which students defended a thesis according to the strict rules of logic. Luther must have been quite adept at this as he acquired his nickname, "the Philosopher," at that time.[3]

Of Luther's Erfurt years we know little. His excellent Eisenach training laid a foundation for educational achievement, and he earned his bachelor of arts degree in 1502 and his master's in 1505. His success paved the way for his eventual appointment to university teaching. Fellow students remembered Luther as a good musician (he sang and played the lute) and a good comrade, although given on occasion to melancholy.

Luther's father was so pleased with his son's progress that he bought him a copy of the *corpus iurus,* the Roman law code. With this gift Hans Luther also celebrated Luther's intention to study law, which he started on May 20, 1505.

The Augustinian Monastery

Shortly after undertaking his law studies, Luther experienced a pivotal event. On the way back to Erfurt after a visit to his parental home, a violent thunderstorm overtook him. Lightning struck so close to Luther that the air pressure hurled him to the ground and he cried out, "Saint Anne, help me. I will become a monk." So, two weeks later, on July 17, Luther sought admission to the Augustinian cloister in Erfurt.

Despite appearances to the contrary, Luther's decision to enter the monastery was neither a sudden decision nor the keeping of a vow made in hasty fright. He never spoke explicitly about this decision, but it appears that an inner struggle consumed him just then. Luther could be impulsive in speech, but he did not make major decisions hastily. The lightning bolt had triggered a decision already in process.

Choosing a monastic vocation was not uncommon in those times. Whenever religion became important to a medieval person, he or she became a monastic. With Luther, however, it went much deeper— God's being gripped him. God stood over against him as Judge and Ruler. God was too real to be ignored. Luther wanted to be a friend of God and to have God as his friend. In 1534 he said in a sermon:

> With reference to my previous experience, I was myself a monk for fifteen years and diligently all through those years read and did everything I could. Yet I was never able to

console myself regarding my baptism, but always thought "Oh, when will you once become pious enough, or do enough to obtain a gracious God?" Such thoughts drove me into the monastery.[4]

It is significant that Luther joined the Augustinians; four other orders had monastic houses in Erfurt. The Augustinian Order was not begun by St. Augustine of Hippo, the early church father whose name it bears. Created in 1256, the order did reflect some of Augustine's teaching and an emphasis on diligent study of the scriptures, along with earnest preaching. At that time the Augustinians enjoyed both strength and popularity. Perhaps some of Luther's university professors were Augustinians, which influenced him toward this order. At any rate, Luther adopted his new vocation with diligence. During his novitiate year, Luther wore the white alb covered with a black mantle. A little black skullcap covered his partly shaved head. This somber attire earned the monastery the title "the Black Cloister."[5]

In obedience to his superiors, Luther was ordained a Roman Catholic priest on April 3, 1507. On May 2, he celebrated his first mass. He was pleased that his father accepted his invitation to attend the latter event; Hans Luther had reacted like a madman to his son's decision to exchange a promising law career for the unproductive life of a monk. He had been counting on Martin as old-age insurance for him and his wife. Hans finally relented, however, and with twenty friends appeared for the first mass. He also made a significant financial contribution to the monastery.

Luther performed his first mass without difficulty, though he did hesitate for a moment when he considered the awfulness of God's majesty and his own unworthiness. At the dinner afterward, he described his way into the ministry, referring to the lightning bolt as "a divine call from heaven." That was too much for his father, who startled everyone by suggesting that it might, instead, have been the work of an evil spirit. He challenged Luther: "Don't you know that it is written, 'Honor thy father and mother'?"[6]

Luther advanced in his theological studies, but he felt he failed in his attempt to please God through monastic rigor. He denied himself food, drink, and sleep; he kept all the prayer vigils and declared, "If ever a monk got to heaven by his monkery, I certainly should have got there." His continued alienation from the God he sought to appease created a spiritual dilemma. If he felt he had met God's holiness requirements, he was tempted to pride; if not, he sank into despair. Luther found himself in a period of great pain and unrest. He experienced *Anfechtung*, which normally is translated "temptation." For him, however, it was much more serious. It connoted a sense of being forsaken by God. He reported, "I was the most miserable man on earth."[7]

Help came to the beleaguered monk through Johann von Staupitz, vicar general of the Augustinian order in Germany. Von Staupitz expressed keen interest both in Luther's problems and possibilities. In appreciation for Von Staupitz's theological and spiritual counsel, Luther later said that without him he would have sunk into the deepest hell.[8]

Von Staupitz, believing that a change of scenery and an even heavier workload would benefit his anxious monk, transferred Luther in 1508 to Wittenberg University, a six-year-old institution boasting only three hundred students. The chief industry of Wittenberg, an unsightly town of two thousand inhabitants, was beer brewing. Years later, Luther admitted that the Wittenbergers "dwell on the outskirts of civilization."[9] A student riot, however, forced his return to Erfurt.

Luther then got the travel opportunity of his life: the privilege of walking to Rome! Von Staupitz was trying to get all twenty-nine of his German cloisters to maintain a uniformly strict observation of the Augustinian rule. The Erfurt cloister refused to comply and dispatched two brothers to Rome to object to Egidio, the general of the order. Luther, who must have agreed with thisobjection, was one of the two chosen. (Clearly his friendship with Von Staupitz was not yet as close as it would later become.)

The trip of November 1510 to March 1511 had no special religious significance for Luther. He admitted later that he had run "like a mad saint through all the churches and crypts." He said mass at a number of altars. As he climbed the Scala Sancta, he offered a prayer on each step so as to redeem his grandfather Heine from purgatory. He later admitted that when he came to the top step, he did question, "Who knows whether it is so?"[10]

The mission failed. General Egidio was unimpressed with the monks' protest. Upon their return, Luther and his colleague persuaded the Erfurt cloister to submit to Von Staupitz's demands.

Professor at Wittenberg University

By late summer of 1511, Luther returned to teaching at Wittenberg University. He received his doctorate in biblical studies on October 19, 1512, and three days later became a university faculty member. Luther now taught holy scripture, as he would for the rest of his life. He emphasized biblical understanding as the foundation on which he based his life and ministry.

All medieval biblical interpreters followed a fourfold approach to scripture. The literal method took the text for what it seemed to be saying; another approach interpreted the text in light of other biblical texts; the third approach tried to identify what the scripture text said for the believer's faith; and the fourth approach conveyed what the text said about last things, or the end of the world. Luther departed from the customary practice of putting every text through this fourfold interpretive sieve. He stressed the literal meaning but, even more, he focused on what the scripture passage said for individual believers and the church.[11] Luther believed that God was speaking to him in the Bible, that the God who acts also speaks from the pages of scripture. The Bible, he contended, contains the word of God, God's gospel in Jesus Christ. Therefore, Christ is the Lord of the Bible, and the books of the Bible are genuine only insofar as they preach Christ. At this point Luther found trouble with the Epistle of James. He believed that it failed to preach Christ as Savior and so was "an epistle full of straw."[12]

For Luther, the word of God was not the Bible or even the words in the Bible. The word was a cry, a message from God, that testified of Christ. Luther called the scriptures "the swaddling clothes and the manger in which Christ lies."[13] Thus, as Luther prepared his classroom lectures, he increasingly ignored the opinions of other theologians and permitted the word of God to address him from the printed page. This change of method in biblical interpretation led to theological change as well.

Despite his increase in biblical knowledge, Luther still had no inner peace, haunted as he was at the thought of an angry, righteous, and demanding God whom he sought in vain to please. The church's theology offered him more bad news than good. A current theological emphasis touted humanity's free will by which persons could perform righteous acts so as to merit God's saving grace. This approach did not work for Luther. Moreover, some persons believed that a leftover spark of the divine in each person made salvation possible if each did the good that lay within him or her; then God would respond with divine grace. The catchword became, "God will not refuse grace to those who do what is within them."[14]

Struggling under a load of guilt, Luther felt all the worse. He wanted to know a merciful God, but his quest seemed futile. His turning toward the sacraments and then to mysticism brought only temporary relief. There remained fixed in his mind since boyhood the stained-glass window in his home church that depicted Christ sitting on a rainbow judging the world. Out of Christ's right ear grew a lily, under which the saved were joyfully entering into heaven; out of his left ear was a sword, under which the damned with tormented faces were falling into hell.[15] Luther was terrified of, and obsessed with, Christ the Judge.

The Tower Discovery

Fortunately, Luther came to his "tower discovery," so named because his study was in the tower of Wittenberg's Augustinian monastery. Scholars argue as to when it happened, for Luther himself never dated it. It quite possibly occurred in 1512–13 when Luther was lecturing on the Psalms. Psalms 31 and 71 forced him to exegete a troubling passage: "Deliver me in thy righteousness." He also encountered in Romans 1:17 Paul's contention that in the gospel "the righteousness of God is revealed through faith for faith."

Luther found the term *the righteousness of God* repulsive. For him it depicted an image of God who judges and punishes unrighteous sinners. Yet Romans 1:17 concluded with the promise that "the one who is righteous will live by faith."

In grappling with these scriptures and his own longings, Luther had a breakthrough:

> Then I began to comprehend "the righteousness of God"
> through which the righteous are saved by God's grace, namely
> through faith; that the "righteousness of God" which is

revealed through the Gospel was to be understood in a passive sense in which God through mercy justifies man by faith, as it is written, "The just shall live by faith." Now I felt exactly as if I had been born again, and I believed that I had entered Paradise through widely opened doors. I then went through the Holy Scriptures as far as I could recall them from memory, and I found in other parts the same sense: the "work of God" is that which he works in us, the "strength of God" is that through which he makes us strong, "the wisdom of God" that through which he makes us wise, and so "the power of God," the "blessing of God," and "the honor of God" are likewise to be interpreted.[16]

Luther never regarded this discovery as an ecstatic experience or a mystical vision. Instead, the gospel-as-good-news became available to him in the pages of holy scripture. The light had broken into his spiritual darkness and forever changed him. Luther would suffer subsequent trials and doubts, but he clung to his central conviction that his efforts could not save him and that he was justified by God's grace alone. As his conviction deepened, Luther persuaded his colleagues on the university theology faculty and a growing number of students into accepting his evangelical position.

The Ninety-Five Theses

Beginning in 1516, Luther undertook pastoral duties at Wittenberg's city church, substituting for the sick parish priest. He heard troubling stories of parishioners crossing over to neighboring Brandenburg, where the Dominican indulgence salesman, Johann Tetzel, was inciting the people to buy his wares. Luther found the practice repugnant and on October 31, 1516, and February 24, 1517, he preached against the abuse of indulgences.

When a copy of Archbishop Albert's instructions for his indulgence salesmen fell into Luther's hands, he decided to act. Albert's letter lauded indulgences as "the inestimable gift of God" for reconciling people to God and emptying purgatory. Luther responded with ninety-five theses in which he contended that Christians should gladly suffer temporal punishment for sin and should not want this indulged. Some of Luther's brief theses questioned the pope's right to extend indulgences to the dead in purgatory. It was at this point that the unscrupulous Tetzel was making his greatest sales and Luther even quoted the popular ditty connected with the indulgence sales: "As soon as the coin in the coffer rings / The soul from purgatory springs."[17] Even though Luther strongly attacked the pope, he also included several affirmations of the pope's authority.

Whether or not Luther nailed the ninety-five theses to the door of the Castle Church in Wittenberg on October 31, 1517, remains a debated question. Since Luther published them in Latin to invite academic debate, he logically would have placed them on the Castle Church door, which served as the university's bulletin board. The timing also would have been perfect since on November 1, All Saints Day, throngs of people would pass through that door to earn indulgences before Frederick the Wise's relic collection.[18] It is known that Luther wisely mailed a copy to his bishop, Archbishop Albert of Mainz.

The immediate response was minimal. The formal academic debate never happened. In a few weeks, however, copies of the theses, now published in German, were circulating widely. Congratulations poured in to Luther, who had apparently spoken for many. People who were anti-Italian, antipapal, anticlerical, anticapitalist, antimonopolistic, and antigovernment responded with what could be translated into folksy North American discourse as "'Atta boy, Monk."[19]

Cries of protest were also raised. The Dominicans rushed to Tetzel's defense. Archbishop Albert's copy of the theses circulated like a political football from the University of Mainz theological faculty, to the curia (papal administration) in Rome, to the Augustinian order. Rome's response to Luther thus took several interesting turns.

The Heidelberg Chapter Meeting

The curia asked Von Staupitz to have Luther appear at the Augustinian chapter meeting in Heidelberg, which occurred on April 25, 1518. There Luther defended another set of theses that never mentioned indulgences, but discussed grace, free will, and faith. In this set Luther introduced his theology of the cross, insisting that God is best revealed not in glory, but in suffering and the cross. Attacking "works righteousness," Luther contended that "he is not righteous who does much, but he who, without work, believes much in Christ."[20]

Several of Luther's former teachers from Erfurt were there. Though cordial, they were unconvinced by Luther. Still, they initiated no action regarding him. The reformer did gain two young men to his cause: Martin Butzer, a Dominican and later the reformer of Strassburg, and Johannes Brenz, a priest who became the chief Lutheran reformer in Southwest Germany. Luther summarized his Heidelberg appearance this way: "I went on foot; I came back in a wagon."

The Augsburg Meeting with Cardinal Cajetan

Theological experts in Rome who looked into Luther's further writings believed he was a heretic. On August 7, 1518, they summoned the professor to Rome for trial in sixty days. Luther appealed to his prince, Frederick the Wise, to have the trial changed to Augsburg where the diet (an assembly of political and religious leaders) would soon be meeting. Frederick easily accomplished this because the papacy still wanted him to become the next emperor. Thus Cardinal Cajetan, the general of the Dominican Order, held a private hearing for Luther.

Cajetan, while initially kind, called on Luther to recant his teaching of new doctrines. Luther defended himself by appealing both to scripture and church law. Cajetan angrily dismissed him. Although Cajetan was a noted scholar, Luther later wrote that he could handle the case about as well as an ass could play the harp! Afraid for the professor's life, Luther's friends sneaked him out of Augsburg to safety, but not before Von Staupitz released him from his vows to the Augustinian order. Frederick the Wise refused Cajetan's insistence that he either turn Luther over to Rome or banish him from Saxony. Luther returned gratefully to Wittenberg.

The Leipzig Debate

Soon afterward came the challenge from the popular Johann Eck, professor at Ingolstadt University, that a debate be held at Leipzig University between him and Luther and his followers. It was scheduled for June 1519. Eck had already published a set of theses against Luther. Luther went to Leipzig accompanied by his faculty colleagues Andreas Bodenstein von Carlstadt, professor of theology; Philip Melanchthon, professor of Greek and theology; and some two hundred students armed with spears.

The opening days of the debate saw the loud, ostentatious Eck dominate Von Carlstadt, who with a weak voice and a poor memory lacked audience appeal. When Luther's turn came, he and Eck assailed each other's ideas tooth and nail. Luther forced Eck to admit that there had been abuses in the indulgence traffic, but Eck emerged the winner. He maneuvered Luther into openly denying that the authority of the pope was necessary for salvation and that church councils could and did err, citing as an example the Council of Constance in its condemnation of John Hus. Eck's chilling response was that these ideas were heresy. Luther was now labeled "the Saxon Hus."

Luther left the debate even more determined to reform church belief. In 1520 he composed three great treatises that further separated him theologically from Rome. That same year Pope Leo X signed a papal bull (a document made official with the affixing of the pope's *bulla* or seal) condemning Luther if he did not recant within sixty days of receiving it. The bull threatened that Luther's writings would be burned, that he would be released to the mercy of the civil authorities, and that all who aided him would be cited for heresy. In response, on December 10 in front of the faculty and student body at Wittenberg, Luther publicly burned his copy of the papal bull. The students celebrated. From across the adjoining states came the word that many uneducated German people expressed support for the fearless monk who defied the papacy. Rome responded by issuing the bull of excommunication against Luther on January 2, 1521. He was now outside the church.

The Diet of Worms

The imperial diet was scheduled to meet at the city of Worms in January 1521. The pope wanted the emperor to condemn Luther, but Frederick the Wise had earlier wrested assurance from Charles V that no German citizen would be condemned without a hearing. Thus Charles V was forced to grant Luther a public hearing before the diet.

Cardinal Girolamo Aleander, the papal messenger, wanted no hearing and sought to influence the emperor to renege on his promise of safe conduct for Luther. Worms was filled with intrigue.

Aleander found his cool reception unsettling. He had difficulty finding lodging; sarcastic poems ridiculing him and the pope seemed everywhere; men grimaced and reached for their swords when they encountered him. He wrote to the pope, "Nine-tenths of the people are shouting 'Luther,' and the other tenth shouts: 'Down with Rome!'"[21]

Once summoned, Luther took fourteen days to travel from Wittenberg to Worms. Along the way, he preached at Erfurt and Eisenach to packed churches. His good friend Nicholas von Amsdorf and others accompanied him. He resisted the fears of his friends and a last ploy by the emperor's people to dissuade him from attending the diet. He insisted, "Indeed, Christ is alive, and I shall enter Worms in spite of the gates of hell and the powers of darkness."[22] When the Luther party arrived at 10:00 A.M. on April 16, 1521, it received a triumphal escort of one hundred horsemen. An estimated two thousand people thronged the streets to glimpse the new celebrity.

The next afternoon at four o'clock, Luther appeared before the waiting assembly in one of history's dramatic confrontations. Charles V, ruler of much of Europe, with the nobility and bishops of his realm, waited to hear this miner's son, who had been a virtual unknown four years earlier. A pile of books lay on a table, and the archbishop's spokesperson asked Luther a double-barreled question: "Are these your writings, and are you prepared to revoke the heresies they contain?" Luther's lawyer asked that the titles be read. Luther admitted the twenty-five titles were all his, but since these works contained such important issues as God's word, faith, and salvation, he requested an additional day to ponder his answer! The emissaries from Rome were furious, but Charles V granted Luther's request.

On April 18 at 6:00 P.M., Luther entered the meeting in a larger and even more crowded hall connected with the cathedral at Worms.

Again, the official asked the two questions. Luther's reply was long and drawn out, delivered in both Latin and German. Charles V fell asleep during the discourse, although the day before he had muttered, "This monk shall not make me a heretic." Luther said that his writings were not all the same. Some dealt with faith, some with the desolation of the Christian world by the teaching of the papists (here he talked of the incredible tyranny Rome had exercised over the German nation), and some were indeed attacks on individuals. He regretted if he had spoken too vehemently, but, he reminded his audience, he was defending not himself but Christ's teachings. The official impatiently asked Luther how he dared to believe that he alone could interpret scripture. Besides, the emperor wanted an unevasive answer: Would he recant his errors? Luther said in a clear voice:

> Unless I am convinced by the testimonies of the Holy Scriptures or evident reason (for I believe neither in the Pope nor councils alone, since it has been established that they have often erred and contradicted themselves), I am bound by the Scriptures adduced by me, and my conscience has been taken captive by the Word of God, and I am neither able nor willing to recant, since it is neither safe nor right to act against conscience. God help me. Amen.[23]

Whether or not the reformer added the words, "Here I stand, I cannot do otherwise," is uncertain. Those words do not constitute part of the original record. Perhaps the historian Roland Bainton correctly suggested that they may have been spoken but lost from the record because for the moment the auditors may have been too moved to write.[24]

When Luther finished, pandemonium broke out in the hall. Some of the Spaniards hissed, "To the fire with him!" Luther, passing to his friends, lifted his arms above his head like a victorious knight and shouted, "I am through; I am through." Frederick the Wise lived up to his name once again. Asked what he felt about Luther's reply, he said simply, "The professor has spoken boldly, hasn't he?" In his private hearing before the archbishop of Trier the next day, Luther again promised recantation only if scripture forced him to do so.

Charles V declared that he intended to be the protector of the Roman Catholic church and would thus have nothing to do with the Lutheran heresy, which he planned to suppress. Yet he had to move slowly because he needed German support in his coming war with France. He refused to sign Aleander's draft of the Edict of Worms, which condemned Luther, until he got his promised military resources. When on May 25, 1521, the Edict was signed, only a few bishops and princes were still present. Frederick the Wise had already gone home. Yet the Edict's terms were threatening: Luther could be killed on sight. No one was to have anything to do with him, and no one was to read or possess his writings. Forever after, Luther would be safe only in the territory of his supportive prince, Frederick the Wise, and Frederick's successors.

The Wartburg

Luther and Von Amsdorf, under the protection of the imperial herald, left Worms on April 26. Several days later some mounted knights appeared at dusk in the Thuringian forest. "Kidnapping" Luther, they took him to the nearby Wartburg Castle. Now dressed in knight's clothes, Luther became a curly-haired, black-bearded knight called "Junker Jeorg." Frederick the Wise's careful precautions had worked perfectly.

While the European rumor mill worked overtime with unfounded speculation regarding Luther's whereabouts, he made excellent use of his enforced quiet. In eleven weeks he translated the New Testament from Greek and Hebrew into German. Published in September of 1522, this German-language New Testament sold two hundred thousand copies over the next twelve years. The prefaces Luther wrote for many of the New Testament books, as well as the woodcuts that vividly illustrated them, enhanced the value of this translation.

Luther's use of the court language of Saxony for his translation made it understandable in both North and South Germany. The High German that began to be spoken and written as a result of his translation made him, in fact, the author of the modern German language.

Turmoil in Wittenberg

While Luther busied himself with scholarly labors at the Wartburg, his followers at Wittenberg were not idle. Under Von Carlstadt's (a faculty member at Wittenberg) leadership and aided by laymen from nearby Zwickau who felt a keen sense of the Holy Spirit's leading, a tumultuous mood gripped the town. Disturbance and riot took place with some destruction in the city church. The city council was helpless to quell the situation.

On March 6, 1522, Luther defied Frederick the Wise's orders and hurried to Wittenberg. On the following Sunday he began an eight-day sermon series that quelled the riots and rebellious excitement. He averred that preaching, not physical destruction or force of arms, would be the mode of reformation. "The Word will do it," Luther said:

> In short, I will preach it, teach it, write it, but I will constrain no man by force, for faith must come freely without compulsion. Take myself as an example. I opposed indulgences and all the papists, but never with force. I simply taught, preached, and wrote God's Word; otherwise I did nothing. And while I slept (cf. Mark 4:26–29) or drank Wittenberg

beer with my friends Philip and Amsdorf, the Word so greatly weakened the papacy that no prince or emperor ever inflicted such losses upon it. I did nothing; the Word did everything. Had I desired to foment trouble, I could have brought great bloodshed upon Germany; indeed, I could have started such a game that even the emperor would not have been safe. But what would it have been? Mere fool's play. I did nothing; I let the Word do its work.[25]

Luther successfully persuaded the Wittenbergers to stress faith and love, which are "musts," but to allow freedom in secondary issues like eating meat on Friday, venerating images, or even exchanging celibacy for marriage. The breach between him and his former colleague Von Carlstadt widened, resulting in the latter's departure from Wittenberg. Luther's conservatism is evident also in the liturgies he developed in the 1520s; in these he retained much of the Catholic tradition, such as candles, vestments, chants, and organ music. His reform affected mainly the theology being preached and sung in the new hymns and chorales he and others were writing.

Times of Testing

Besides earning the implacable opposition of pope and emperor, Luther's movement now began to suffer defection from groups once inclined to support it. The first of these was a group of knights who graciously had offered Luther asylum or even their swords. Their disastrous war in 1522 against the archbishop of Trier, however, resulted in their death or banishment.

Another group included those Luther called the spiritualists or the "heavenly prophets." These were people given to claiming direct revelations from the Holy Spirit. Luther believed that the Holy Spirit spoke solely through the written word. Von Carlstadt became a leader among the spiritualists, as did a one-time Lutheran and now revolutionary named Thomas Münzer. Von Carlstadt published against Luther, who insisted that his former colleague lived and ministered as if he had "devoured the Holy Spirit feathers and all."[26] Münzer referred to Luther as "Brother Fattened Swine" and "Brother Soft Life" because the reformer opposed his revolutionary advocacy of the sword to usher in the kingdom. Luther unfairly lumped Von Carlstadt and Münzer together under the title "Schwärmer," suggesting that they were swarming about like bees. By 1525 the break between Luther and the spiritualists was complete.

It was at this time that the Erasmus-Luther literary debate occurred, resulting in the humanist withdrawal of support for Luther's Reformation. More will be said about this later in the chapter.

The Peasants' War

The last segment of his followers to renounce Luther consisted of thousands of German peasants. Although the peasants were never well-organized, the fiery preaching of Thomas Münzer inflamed them. He called them to strike their enemies and to show no mercy toward the villains who had oppressed them.[27] The peasants' well-timed rebellion of 1524–25 was another attempt to redress their grievances. Many German princes and their troops were in Italy fighting the French. Armed with pitchforks, scythes, and axes, the peasant armies committed outrages and killed some people, but mostly they captured castles and monasteries, the latter of which had cellars well stocked with good food and wine. The war ended at the Battle of Frankenhausen on May 15, 1525, when an imperial army, just back from Italy, overcame the peasants, killing about five thousand of them in just a few hours.

Consequently Münzer, who had promised the peasants divine protection from enemy swords and bullets, was captured, tortured, and executed. A total of one hundred thousand peasants lost their lives in the war. The survivors were forced to endure three more centuries of injustice.

Luther could not escape commentary on this dangerous situation. He could hardly have been expected to side with the peasants. Already in 1523 he had written, following Romans 13:1, that God had instituted government and permitted disobedience only if a prince commanded something against God or insisted that people fight in an unjust war. Christians, Luther wrote, live in both the kingdom of God where love rules and in the secular realm where laws and force are necessary to keep peace and restrain evil. Christians have to be willing to suffer injustice in the secular realm.

In April 1525, when Luther read the peasants' *Twelve Articles,* he responded first by praising the peasants for their biblical foundation and blaming the princes for their plight. He did tell the peasants to drop the name "Christian" if they persisted in plundering and murdering. But then on April 16 he journeyed to Eisleben to visit family and saw firsthand the results of the peasants' raids and plundering. Fueled also by reports of peasant wrongdoing, he returned and published his now infamous *Against the Robbing and Murdering Hordes of Peasants.* In this he accused the peasants of perjury, rebellion, and blasphemy because they called themselves "Christian Brethren." Losing all restraint, Luther wrote, "Therefore, let everyone who can, smite, slay, and stab, secretly or openly, remembering that nothing can be more poisonous, hurtful, or devilish than a rebel. It is just as when one must kill a mad dog; if you do not strike him, he will strike you, and a whole land with you."[28]

The uncontrolled rage in this publication offended Luther's friends and enemies alike. The more moderate piece he published in June still revealed his distaste for mob rule, but it did condemn the princes who were merciless in suppressing the rebellion.

The reformer cannot escape criticism here. He wrote in anger, made erroneous judgments, and too severely advocated the sword in retaliation. Without question, being who he was, he could not have sided with the peasants, especially in their stretching his concept of Christian freedom much further than he intended it to go. Nonetheless, large numbers of South German peasants now turned a deaf ear to his teaching.

Luther's Marriage to Katharine von Bora

Amazingly, in the midst of the furor over his Peasant War responses, Luther married. During his Wartburg stay, when the Augustinian cloister was breaking up and the monks were beginning to marry, he said: "Good heavens! They won't give me a wife."[29] Then, in 1523, he met Katharine von Bora (1499–1552). She was from a good family, but her mother had died when Katharine was young. When her father remarried, he sent her to a convent where her aunt was the abbess. When she and ten other nuns no longer wished to remain monastic, a merchant smuggled them out of the Nimbschen convent in his wagon. He may have hidden them in empty herring barrels. Luther had made the arrangements.

Nine of these ex-nuns came to Wittenberg, where a student wrote, "A wagon load of vestal virgins just came to town, all more eager for marriage than for life. God grant them husbands lest worse befall."[30]

Luther soon found employment or marriage for these women, but he found Katharine difficult to place. She fell in love with Jerome Baumgartner, but his parents rejected her. No ex-nun for a daughter-in-law for them! Luther's intercession with Baumgartner failed. Feeling sorry for Katharine, he sent his friend Von Amsdorf to tell her that one of his preachers, Caspar Glatz, needed a wife. This also backfired. Katharine said she would marry Dr. Von Amsdorf or even Dr. Luther, but Glatz, never! Von Amsdorf reported this to Luther.

Whether or not this was part of Katharine's strategy is unclear. Luther had developed a liking for her, although he thought she was arrogant and outspoken. Once he decided, Luther moved quickly. On June 18, he and Katharine were married in a small private ceremony; the public wedding was held at the city church in Wittenberg two weeks later.

Luther stated that he was not infatuated with Katie, but that he cherished her. He jokingly gave all kinds of unromantic reasons for their marriage: His parents wanted more grandchildren; he did it to spite the devil; it was a testimony to his faith; he needed a housekeeper. Others had different assessments. Some Roman Catholics declared it quite obvious that the Reformation, though couched in theological terms, was really a pretext for Luther to satisfy his sex drive! Erasmus wrote that what the world had taken to be a tragedy turned out to be a comedy, "the end of which was a wedding."[31]

The Luther home was a happy one. The former monk's quarters in the Augustinian cloister that Frederick the Wise had renovated as a parsonage soon housed six children, making it a place of gaiety and singing. Katie was a thoughtful wife and mother. Her wise management of the family finances and her purchase of a farm to augment their income were very beneficial. Luther was a warm and affectionate husband and father. The death of their fourteen-year-old daughter, Magdalena, was a loss from which neither parent fully recovered. Reference to it appears in many of the reformer's letters of consolation to persons who had lost loved ones.[32]

Luther teased Katie constantly, but the affection between them was abiding. Some of his last letters were tender and loving reassurances to her that she need not worry because of his health. Katie herself was a woman of faith. Widowhood was difficult for her, but her dying words were, "I will stick to Christ as a burr to a top coat."[33]

The Spread of Lutheranism

Even though a number of North German princes had instituted Luther's Reformation in their lands, its success was by no means certain. In 1526, the emperor, needing men and money for his wars, agreed to permit each territorial ruler within the empire to deal with the religious question as his conscience under God dictated. This began popularization of the term *Cuius regio, eius religio* ("Whose the region, his the faith"). Princes could now determine whether they and their subjects would be Roman Catholic or Lutheran. In 1529, the Roman Catholic majority repealed this agreement with the emperor's approval. The Lutheran princes retaliated by lodging their *Protestatio* (from which the word *protestant* derives).

In 1530, Charles V was able to attend the imperial assembly for the first time since the meeting at Worms nine years earlier. Lutheranism had grown in the meantime. To settle the religious question, Charles V invited princes representing diverse religious opinions to present them at the diet, which was scheduled to meet in Augsburg.

John the Steadfast, the Saxon prince who replaced Frederick the Wise at the latter's death in 1525, was a devout man who desired a strong statement of faith. Because Luther was under the ban of the empire and dared not leave Saxony, the task of composing the Lutheran confession of faith fell to Luther's trusted lieutenant, Philip Melanchthon. On June 25, 1530, the Augsburg confession was presented to the emperor and the imperial diet in a two-hour reading. It bore the signatures of the princes of five German states and two free cities. Lutheranism now had a definitive statement of faith.

Charles V and the Roman Catholic majority did not accept it, however. Before the diet of Augsburg adjourned, Charles announced that the Lutheran princes had until April 15, 1531, to submit to the Roman church or face military consequences. The Lutherans subsequently organized the Schmalkaldic League for mutual defense. Nothing happened on April 15, 1531, due to a Turkish threat in the east. Luther did not live to see the Schmalkaldic War that occurred the year after his death.

Between the early 1520s and the late 1530s, Lutheranism spread to Denmark, Sweden, Norway, Finland, and Iceland. This occurred largely through acts of the crown and also due to the ministries of intrepid Scandinavian preachers, often Wittenberg-trained. Lutheranism also entered Hungary, Poland, Latvia, and Estonia through German traders and settlers.

Luther's Last Years

For the rest of his life, Luther was the heart and soul of the Reformation he had inadvertently begun. He attracted hundreds of ministerial candidates to study under him at Wittenberg. His *Small Catechism* for laypersons and his *Large Catechism* for pastors (both published in 1529) reveal his concern to teach the church, as do his many biblical commentaries and published sermons.

Luther marred his late years by publishing a vitriolic book against the Jews in 1543. Once open and conciliatory toward the Jews, Luther had invited a rabbi to aid in the translation of the Old Testament into German he and others published in 1534. His later severe judgments, however, stemmed from the Jews' not converting to his brand of

Christianity and their maintaining a religion of legalism (salvation by works) that he saw in Roman Catholicism, Islam, and some Protestants. Nonetheless, his intolerance was most unfortunate. He did recommend that Jews not be harmed physically, but in the twentieth century the Nazis used lengthy sections of his *On the Jews and Their Lies* for their diabolical purposes.

In February 1546, against Katie's wishes, Luther journeyed to Eisleben to help arbitrate among the counts of Mansfeld, whose financial policies adversely affected some of his own family members. The presence of his three sons and his close friend, Justus Jonas, comforted him. Stricken with a heart attack at the end of the negotiations, he died peacefully about 2:45 A.M. on February 18, 1546. His body was returned to Wittenberg and laid to rest under the pulpit of the Castle Church there.

Luther, a complicated man, could approach the sublime in describing Christian salvation, but he could also use coarse language in order to refute his opponents. His friend Philip Melanchthon, in his funeral oration, lauded Luther's tremendous gifts and accomplishments but did not overlook his faults, saying, "God gave this last age a sharp physician on account of its great sickness."[34]

LUTHER'S UNDERSTANDING OF THE CHRISTIAN FAITH

Luther's understanding of the faith can best be summarized by a glance at his three great treatises of 1520 and at what he considered one of his best publications, his reply to Erasmus entitled *On the Bondage of the Will.*

The first great treatise of 1520 entitled *Address to Christian Nobility of the German Nation*[35] appeared in August of that year. The four thousand copies first published sold out in two weeks. Written in German, the treatise was a powerful appeal to German nationalism. In it the reformer attacked the three walls behind which he believed the papacy had entrenched itself. The first of these was that the pope was above all temporal interest and that laity had no involvement in church reform. Luther believed in the "two realms"—the church, which would care for persons' souls, and the state, which would look after their temporal interests. Therefore, the state was endowed with the sword to protect its subjects from evil.

Luther denied that spiritual power was superior to temporal power. All baptized Christians were equal. There was no such thing as a "secular estate" and a "spiritual estate." All Christians belonged to the royal priesthood and God wished to extend divine love through all of them to one another. To be sure, Christian congregations could not have every member preaching and administering the sacraments. For purposes of order they must single out their most gifted and pious members. Such persons would differ from all the rest, not in rank, but in office. All Christians belonged to the priesthood and could glorify God in their callings. Milkmaids and carters of manure could do so in their daily labors as much as priests, nuns, and monks.

The second wall was the idea that the pope alone could interpret scripture. Luther's priesthood-of-all-believers idea insisted that, by the inspiration of the Holy Spirit, each Christian could understand the scriptures. Luther admitted that this was more difficult and that trained theologians and pastors were better equipped to understand the scriptures than simple laypersons were. Still, the scriptures were to be available to all.

The third wall was the fact that only a pope could call a general council. The priesthood of all believers gave that right to all Christians, said Luther, especially those in positions of political power. The emperor was equal in this regard with the pope. If the latter did not act to reform the church, the former had every right and responsibility to do so. After all, the Emperor Constantine called the first great ecumenical council at Nicaea. When the pope seeks to prevent reform he becomes an instrument of the devil and the Antichrist.Luther concluded his treatise by imploring the nobles to effect a number of political and social reforms as well as religious ones.

In October 1520, Luther's second treatise, *The Babylonian Captivity of the Church,* appeared. Written in Latin, it was intended only for scholars and clergy. Its thesis was that the souls of the German people were in bondage to the papal sacramental system. Luther broke the bondage by eliminating four of the sacraments (marriage, ordination, confirmation, and extreme unction) because scripture did not support their institution by Christ. Penance was retained for some years because of the values of contrition and confession, but clerical absolution for sin was dropped. No one but God, he maintained, could forgive sin.

Luther had much to say regarding the Lord's Supper or Eucharist. He believed that the medieval church had committed three errors regarding it. The first was that the church had denied the laity the cup. Luther quoted Matthew 26:27 where our Lord told the apostles, "Drink from it, all of you." If the sacrament in one kind was not complete for priests, Luther reasoned, neither was it so for the laity. Cyprian, bishop of Carthage in the third century, reported that the sacrament was administered in both kinds to the laity, even to children. Scripture and tradition alike call for the cup for the laity.

Luther found the second error to be the doctrine of transubstantiation. To be sure, Christ's real flesh and blood were present in the Eucharist but not because the bread and wine were changed in substance. Scripture never mentioned any substantial change in the bread and wine. Why could not Christ's body be in the outward form of the bread and wine as well as in the substance or the inner reality without changing the latter? Fire and iron could become thoroughly intermingled without a change to either. Luther admitted that he could not explain it, but he knew that the body of Christ was in the bread and the bread in the body of Christ.

Luther's third and most serious objection to the medieval church's doctrine was that it called the mass a sacrifice of Christ on the altar and a good work done by priest and people alike. To Luther the Lord's Supper was not a human action but a testament, a promise of what God in Christ does for the forgiveness of sins. A testament involves two things: the death of the testator (the one making the last will and testament) and the promise of the inheritance with the naming of the heirs. That is what Christ did in the upper room, Luther insisted, waxing eloquent: "For where there is the Word of the promising God, there must necessarily be the faith of the accepting man. It is plain, therefore, that the beginning of our salvation is a faith which clings to the Word of the promising God, who, without any effort on our part, in free and unmerited mercy takes the initiative and offers us the word of his promise."[36] People come to the table not to give but to receive the sacrament as God's gift; Luther called it "a most lavish banquet"[37] and "a fountain of love."[38]

Baptism is also a testament in which God promises salvation through the washing away of the guilt of original sin. Here and in his *Large Catechism* the reformer deplored Saint Jerome's statement that penance was "the second plank after shipwreck." The ship in this statement represented baptism. It suggested that because people sin after their baptism, penance was the sacrament upon which they need rely most. Luther objected. Baptism, the ship, "remains one, solid, and invincible." People who fell into sin should return to their baptism, which was the enacted promise of God's salvation begun in their lives as infants. One could not lose the salvation granted in baptism unless one refused to believe it. Luther preferred immersion in baptism because that signified our dying and rising with Christ.

Infants should be baptized on the faith of others, argued Luther, just as the paralytic in Mark 2:3–12 was healed on the faith of others. Within a few years, Luther had to defend infant baptism, not from the Roman Catholics, but from the Anabaptists. He likewise denounced rebaptism, which he felt they were practicing. On that occasion he argued, "When faith comes, baptism is complete. A second baptism is not necessary."[39] In *The Babylonian Captivity of the Church,* the reformer also advocated the abolition of all religious vows because they caused monks and nuns to trust in their good works instead of God's grace in baptism.

In November 1520, Luther's third great treatise was published in Latin. He entitled it *The Freedom of a Christian* and dedicated it to Pope Leo X. There is no record that Leo ever read it. It probably would have been difficult for him to read beyond the dedication which flattered him but denounced the church and the Roman leadership in harsh tones. This work was one of Luther's best literary compositions. Basing it on 1 Corinthians 9:19 and Romans 13:8, Luther described the paradoxical nature of Christian freedom. He wrote, "A Christian is a perfectly free lord of all, subject to none. A Christian is a perfectly dutiful servant of all, subject to all."[40]

It was clear to the reformer that our good works would never make us right with God. That could transpire only in the soul by faith. Again, Luther stressed the importance of the word of God, here described as "the Gospel of God concerning his Son, who was made flesh, suffered, rose from the dead, and was glorified through the Spirit who sanctifies." Immediately thereafter, Luther said that "faith alone is the saving and efficacious use of the Word of God."[41] Thus Christ, or the message of and about Christ, is the saving Word from God. Salvation comes only as it is believed. Faith frees us from trying to appease God by doing the work of the law. It also saves us from death and damnation. It so relieves our burden that it makes us feel as if we are free lords or kings. Faith likewise honors God and unites us with Christ. Because faith is located within, *being* is more important than *doing*.

This is not irresponsible freedom, however. Good works, which can in no wise help us achieve our salvation, are necessary. Being freed from self-concern by faith, we now can turn to our neighbor in love. Luther urged us "to give ourselves as a Christ to our neighbors, just as Christ has offered himself to us." He put it succinctly: "We conclude, therefore, that a Christian lives not in himself, but in Christ and in his neighbor. Otherwise he is not a Christian. He lives in Christ through faith, in his neighbor through love. By faith, he is caught up beyond himself into God. By love he descends beneath himself into his neighbor."[42] Faith frees people; love binds them as servants.

Luther's next significant work, his reply to the great humanist Erasmus, was a response to the latter's book, *On the Freedom of the Will.* Published in 1524, Erasmus's book insisted that through the fall of Adam and Eve the human will, though wounded by sin, had not been extinguished or destroyed. Erasmus defined it carefully: "By free choice in this place we mean the power of the human will by which a man can apply himself to the things which lead to human salvation, or turn away from them."[43]

Erasmus was impressed by the many allusions to human choice recorded in scripture, and preeminently by our Lord's weeping over Jerusalem (Matt. 23:37) and lamenting how he would have gathered her children together as a hen collects her chicks under her wing, but the city was unwilling. Thus, Erasmus believed, one should champion freedom of the human will. Thereby one could justly blame those lost persons who had spitefully resisted God's grace, could thus avoid attributing cruelty and injustice to God, could escape both despair and a false sense of security, and could be stimulated in the doing of good works.[44] Erasmus used telling illustrations, such as the one in which a father places an apple on a table before his son who is unable to walk and then supports the child's faltering steps until he reaches the apple as a reward.[45] Erasmus taught that people could not receive salvation on their own. For this their free wills needed the assistance of God's grace.

In 1525 Luther responded to Erasmus with *On the Bondage of the Will.* He thanked Erasmus for bypassing themes like indulgences and the papacy and getting to the heart of the matter, the nature and destiny of humankind. There all agreement ended, however. Erasmus early on had stated his preference for the skeptic's approach over making assertions. Luther could hardly resist comment. His response demonstrated the methodological difference between the two scholars. Luther retorted, "Nothing is better known or more common among Christians than assertion. Take away assertions and you take away Christianity."[46] Besides, "The Holy Spirit is no skeptic."[47]

The men also quarreled, via the pen, regarding scripture. Erasmus confessed that we would do better not to penetrate many puzzling things in scripture.[48] Luther agreed but contended that the basic gospel of Jesus Christ was clearly manifest for people to believe.[49]

Using Romans 3, Luther insisted that the natural person is not free but a slave to sin. Of course, people have freedom in "things below": what to eat or drink, whether or not to marry, what vocation to enter. When it comes to "things above," their salvation, however, they must trust in an all-wise God. His main point was that in salvation, it is God, not humanity, who has free will. God alone directs the universe; God is life-giving will. God does not will a thing because it is right; it is right because God has willed it. There is a divine determinism to the universe. God is not the author of sin but will use sin to fulfill the divine purpose, just as a farmer will drive a lame horse along with sound ones.[50]

The human soul is not free in matters of salvation. It is like a beast of burden. Either God or Satan will ride.[51] As to all the apparent free-choice scriptural passages Erasmus quoted, Luther brushed them aside, stating that they really did not promise free will. They only indicated how little humanity, left to its own devices, is able to accomplish. Luther then played his trump card, arguing in effect, "If free will needs to be assisted by grace, just how free is it?"[52]

Erasmus and Luther did not always refute each other's claims. Erasmus, perhaps, appeals more to the modern mind with his concern to defend the goodness and justice of God, as well as human freedom. Luther, much more impressed with humanity's inability than its ability, preferred to extol the power of God. Writing more from a position of vital faith than from skepticism, he thundered at Erasmus: "These words of yours, devoid of Christ, devoid of the Spirit, are colder than ice itself."[53] It is rationally more satisfying to contend that we have human freedom, even in our relationship with God. Careful observation of what we do with our free choice is not so reassuring, however. It drives us to place our faith in God's grace much more than in our limited and tired capacities.

Luther's view of the Christian life has much to commend it. He speaks to the issues that confront people today. His theology focuses on God and not on ourselves—a necessary corrective to our age so soaked in self-help and self-evaluation. A British Methodist theologian, Philip S. Watson, in 1947 published his treatment of Luther's theology under the fetching title, *Let God Be God.* Watson credited Luther with creating a Copernican revolution in religion. Just as the sixteenth-century Polish astronomer, Nicolaus Copernicus, had proved that we live in a sun-centered universe and not an earth-centered one, so Luther caused a similar revolution in matters of faith. He called on people to have a God-centered faith based on God's nature, promises, and actions rather than a human-centered faith that focuses on our frail efforts at self-realization and self-justification before God.[54] A refreshing freedom comes in letting God save us by divine grace rather than believing that we have to measure up to some impossible standard.

The drastic change in Luther's life came about as he studied the holy scriptures. They portrayed to him a God he need not seek, but the God who was seeking him. Luther beautifully illustrates the profound truth that when overwhelmed by spiritual problems, people do far better to focus on God than to wallow in self-pity and self-interest. Always willing to overstate matters to make a point, Luther once said that Christians who focus on their feelings are likely to lose Christ.[55]

The reformer was speaking out of his own experience. Far from fearing a God who stood over him in harsh condemnation and whom he sought in vain to please by doing good works, he came to see God as "a glowing furnace of love."[56] To be sure, God is almighty so as to command our adoration, but also loving so as to arouse our trust and gratitude. For this reason, people are saved when they respond to God's grace in Christ by faith alone.

Another aspect of Luther's theology was its Christ-centeredness. Thanks to his emphasis on salvation by grace through faith, Luther warned against making Christ into another Moses, a lawgiver, a taskmaster.[57] To be sure, Christians ought to follow their Lord's example, but they can do this only when they first fully receive him as their Savior.[58] In *The Freedom of a Christian,* the German reformer went so far as to say that faith unites us with Christ. To illustrate this he suggested that Christ and a believer are related to one another as are a bridegroom and bride. As in every marriage, the two partners bring gifts to one another. For Luther, the soul (the bride) brings sin, death, and damnation, which Christ (the bridegroom) takes upon himself. In return he offers grace, life, and salvation. Faith is the wedding ring. As Christ and the soul make this dowry exchange, Christ accepts and swallows up the soul's burdens.[59]

Quite naturally, Luther focused on Christ's death on the cross for our salvation. For this reason he could write, "Faith, therefore, does not originate in works; neither do works create faith, but faith must spring up and flow from the blood and wounds and death of Christ."[60] Luther would have highly approved of Augustus Toplady's immortal lines:

> Nothing in my hand I bring,
> Simply to thy cross I cling;
> Naked, come to thee for dress;
> Helpless, look to thee for grace;
> Foul, I to thy fountain fly;
> Wash me, Savior, or I die.

A third contribution to spiritual life lay in the vital way in which Luther described faith. Most Methodist Christians have heard John Wesley's well-known account of his life-changing spiritual experience in 1738. His journal entry for May 24 of that year contains these words:

> In the evening I went very unwillingly to a society in Aldersgate Street, where one was reading Luther's preface to the Epistle to the Romans. About a quarter before nine, while he was describing the change which God works in the heart through faith in Christ, I felt my heart strangely warmed. I felt I did trust in Christ, Christ alone for salvation; and an assurance was given me that He had taken away *my* sins, even *mine*, and saved *me* from the law of sin and death.[61]

Wesley never stated which of Luther's words in this brief preface the Holy Spirit used that night to address him in his need. One can well imagine that it was the reformer's contention that we are expected to fulfill the law of God with loving hearts, but this is impossible unless the Holy Spirit places this love into our hearts. The Holy Spirit comes, however, only "in, with, and through faith in Jesus Christ." Faith comes only through the word of God, the gospel. With glowing words Luther described faith in the Christian life:

> Faith, however, is something that God effects in us. It changes us and we are reborn from God (John 1:13). Faith puts the old Adam to death and makes us quite different men in heart, in mind, and in all our powers; and it is accompanied by the Holy Spirit. O, when it comes to faith, what a living, creative, active, powerful thing it is.... Faith is a living and unshakeable confidence, a belief in the grace of God so assured that a man would die a thousand deaths for its sake. This kind of confidence in God's grace, this sort of knowledge of it, makes us joyful, high-spirited, and eager in

our relations with God and with all mankind....Hence, the man of faith, without being driven, willingly and gladly seeks to do good to everyone, serve everyone, suffer all kinds of hardships, for the sake of the love and glory of the God who has shown him such grace.[62]

Wesley had gone to this London society meeting distressed about his soul and his ministry. Luther's stirring words must have challenged him to lay aside his desire to make himself right with God through self-discipline and good works. Instead, he heard that only by the invasion of God's grace could a person be turned from doubt and despair to faith.

Although he did not precisely mention it in his *Preface to the Epistle of St. Paul to the Romans,* the reformer frequently quoted Matthew 8:13 where our Lord told the centurion, "Go; let it be done for you according to your faith." Luther was fond of saying, *"So glaubst du, so hast du"* ("As you believe, so you have"). He was convinced that the truly rich people in the world were those who trust God's promises in Christ. People who believe that God is filled with wrath will come to experience what they believe even if their premise is not true. Luther's words depict how it is not our faith in faith but our trust in God that makes all the difference. He explained, "However, the other thought, that God is gracious to sinners who feel their sins, is simply true and remains so. You should not suppose that it will be this way because you believe this way. Rather be sure that a thing which is sure and true of itself becomes more sure and true when you believe it."[63]

Faith is the only way to receive grace. The "haves" of this world, for Luther, were those who pinned all their hopes and expectations on the divine word, the promises of God to us in Jesus Christ.

Another contribution of Luther's was the place he made for joy. He who himself had once labored under what he considered the law's demands, eventually knew the heartening release of living under God's grace in Christ. Luther spoke of joy in the Christian life partly because he was blessed with a great sense of humor. He also believed that our salvation in Christ moves us from cowering under life's burdens to celebrating the assurance that God's grace in Christ frees us from the heavy anxieties and fears of daily existence. Luther, an honest man, was subject to cloudy and depressive thoughts. Thus, when he wrote a fellow clergyman quoting Proverbs 17:22, "A cheerful heart is a good medicine, but a downcast spirit dries up the bones," he admitted that he was sharing his advice but not taking it himself![64]

Still, Luther's letters were filled with appeals for joyous living because we belong to Christ. In 1531 Luther wrote a touching letter to his aged mother, who was near death. He sought to tie joy to faith.

Therefore, let us rejoice with all assurance and gladness. Should any thought of sin or death frighten us, let us lift up our hearts and say: "Behold, dear soul, what are you doing? Dear death, dear sin, how is it that you are alive and terrify me? Do you not know that you have been overcome? Do you, death, not know that you are quite dead? Do you not know the One who has said of you, 'I have overcome the world'? It does not behoove me to listen to or heed your terrifying suggestions. I shall pay attention only to the cheering words of my Savior, 'Be of good cheer . . . , I have overcome the world' (John 16:33). He is the Conqueror, the true Hero, who in these words, 'Be of good cheer', gives me the benefit of his victory. I shall cling to him. To his words and comfort I shall hold fast. Whether I remain here or go yonder, he will not forsake me."[65]

Not only in life's extremities but also in its daily round the reformer saw the clear connection between faith and love—and the joy that results in Christian living when people live freely under God's grace in Christ. In one of his best sermons, entitled *On the Sum of the Christian Life,* he affirmed:

> For the man who through faith is sure in his heart that he has a gracious God, who is not angry with him, though he deserves wrath, that man goes out and does everything joyfully. Moreover, he can live this way before men also, loving and doing good to all, even though they are not worthy of love. Toward God, therefore, he stands in a relationship of certainty that he is secure for Christ the Mediator's sake, that he does not wish to cast him into hell, but rather lovingly smiles upon him and opens heaven for him.
>
> This is the highest security, the head and foundation of our salvation. Accordingly, I go out to my neighbor with my life and do the best I can for him as my office or station requires or commands. And when I do less than is right, I go to him first and ask him to forgive me.[66]

Like many people, Luther's behavior did not always reflect his theology. Still, his discovery in scripture that people by God's grace can have a right relationship with God vastly changed his outlook on life. Having that fundamental relationship secured, he believed that a joyful and loving life would follow.

Interestingly, during a period in 1527 when he suffered from dizziness and from a disease occasioned both by high fever and physical weakness, Luther succumbed to a feeling of psychological abandonment. The prayers of his wife and friends sustained him in his despair. During this time he composed his majestic hymn, "A Mighty Fortress Is Our God." A clue to his personal faith lay in his admission that "the prince of darkness grim" was raging in his life. Luther surmounted these personally trying times with the assurance that he need not fear the devil's onslaughts because "one little Word shall fell him." That Word is Jesus Christ. The reformer came through his own rough moments by naming and clinging to Jesus Christ.[67]

A PRAYER OF MARTIN LUTHER

Beyond, Lord, an empty vessel that needs to be filled. My Lord, fill it. I am weak in the faith; strengthen thou me. I am cold in love; warm me and make me fervent that my love may go out to my neighbor. I do not have a strong and firm faith; at times I doubt and am unable to trust thee altogether. O Lord, help me. Strengthen my faith and trust in thee. In thee I have sealed the treasures of all I have. I am poor; thou art rich and didst come to be merciful to the poor. I am a sinner; thou art upright. With me there is an abundance of sin; in thee is the fulness of righteousness. Therefore, I will remain with thee of whom I can receive but to whom I may not give. Amen.[68]

1. What is most significant for you about the life story of Martin Luther? In what ways did he most clearly reflect for you the meaning of Christian discipleship?

2. Why was Luther able to attract such a loyal following? Why was he able to influence the church in such a dramatic way?

3. Can you identify with Luther's struggle to experience a merciful God—and not a God of judgment? In what way does this issue touch your faith?

4. As you reflect on Luther's words at Worms, what insights do they offer you about your Christian life and witness?

5. Do you agree with Luther that the word of God is God's message or cry to us? How have you experienced scripture in this way?

6. How would you explain to someone that Christians are saved by grace through faith?

7. Do you agree that the Lord's Supper is not a good thing we do or a commitment we make, as much as it is a gift we freely receive? Do you experience it as a gift? In what way?

8. What is your understanding of baptism and its meaning for the believer?

9. Luther was much opposed to "works righteousness"—the attempt to do the best we can so that God will look favorably on us. Where do you see "works righteousness" in the church today? How does it express itself?

10. Why do we have such difficulty letting God be God in our lives?

UŁRICH
ZWINGŁI

CHAPTER 2

"Not to Fear Is the Armor"

THE LIFE AND MINISTRY
OF ULRICH ZWINGLI

hile Luther was disturbing the peace of church and empire in Germany, another reform voice was rising in Switzerland. As far back as 1291, when several cantons (states) signed a "Perpetual Covenant" of mutual defense, the Swiss had begun severing their ties with the Holy Roman Empire. The half-legendary William Tell was part of this struggle for independence.[1] The Treaty of Basel in 1499 made Switzerland a free nation of thirteen cantons.

Because its thin soil left this Alpine nation economically poor, many of its young men became mercenary soldiers who fought for other powers, particularly France and the papacy. They ran the risk of death or permanent disability, but the fortunate survivors often returned with wages and booty far in excess of a peasant's or mechanic's lifetime wages.

Swiss soldiers were among Europe's finest. They were already being used to guard the Vatican in Rome. Their ranks of massed pikemen stood fast like armed walls against attack by mounted knights. Although in the late Middle Ages artillery had become so effective that sometimes the Swiss in their closed ranks could now be slaughtered, the report still circulated throughout Europe that Swiss soldiers could turn back anything but French gold!

THE LIFE STORY OF ULRICH ZWINGLI

One of the patriotic voices raised against the luring away of his countrymen as "hired guns" was that of Ulrich Zwingli, a young humanist priest. Born on January 1, 1484, in Wildhaus, a village in the Toggenburg valley about forty miles southeast of Zurich, Zwingli came from a good home. Though of peasant stock, his family represented the best qualities of Swiss life—sturdy independence, strong patriotism, and a zeal for religion and scholarship.[2] Zwingli's grandfather and father had been chief magistrates of their shepherd community. The Zwingli children, eight boys and three girls, were happy, well fed, and healthy. The house in which they grew up still stands. The piety of the Zwingli home is evident in the fact that three sons and two daughters entered religious orders.[3]

An exceptionally bright child, Ulrich was sent at age six to live nearby with his uncle Bartholomew, a priest from whom he received a good elementary education. From ages ten to thirteen he attended a secondary school in Basel, followed by two years in Bern. There, under the tutelage of the excellent schoolmaster Heinrich Wolflin, Zwingli pursued a solid humanist and musical foundation. Because of his beautiful singing voice the Dominicans wanted him to join their order. His parents' and uncle's intervention prevented his becoming a Dominican monk.[4]

In 1498 Zwingli matriculated at Vienna University and probably studied there with some interruptions for about three and a half years. While little information remains concerning his studies, we do know that his student friends included Joachim von Watt (Vadianus), later the reformer of Saint Gall; Johann Eck (Luther's later protagonist), and Johann Faber, who eventually became Zwingli's leading Roman Catholic opponent.[5]

Zwingli completed his university studies at Basel, receiving his bachelor's degree in 1504 and his master's degree two years later. There the exciting lectures of Thomas Wittenbach introduced Zwingli and his new friend, Leo Juda, to the New Testament and especially the Epistle to the Romans. Zwingli later said that Wittenbach aroused in him a recognition that "the death of Christ alone is the price of the forgiveness of sins."[6]

Glarus

At the age of twenty-two, Zwingli was ordained a Roman Catholic priest. In the autumn of 1506 he was assigned to be parish priest in Glarus, a town of some thirteen hundred people southwest of Wildhaus. In addition to his pastoral duties, Zwingli started a Latin school for the most able boys in his parish. He had already thrown himself into the study of Greek. The publication in 1516 of Erasmus's Greek New Testament would augment his zeal. Zwingli valued this work from which he hand copied and memorized Paul's epistles. His personal visit with Erasmus increased in Zwingli the humanist's love of scholarship. For some years he maintained a highly prized correspondence with Erasmus.[7]

During his Glarus ministry, Zwingli traveled twice to Italy as chaplain to the local Swiss mercenaries who were fighting for the pope. By 1510 Zwingli already had published an antimercenary tract entitled *The Fable of the Ox*. It warned his countrymen to stay at home or to fight only for the papacy. Zwingli now received a papal pension for his chaplaincy services. It appalled him, however, to see six thousand Swiss troops slaughtered at the Battle of Marignano in 1515. Upon his return home the socially sensitive young priest published *The Labyrinth,* which denounced Swiss willingness to exchange young men for French gold. The hostility aroused by this publication and Zwingli's anti-French preaching helped bring his Glarus ministry to an end.

Einsiedeln

In April 1516 Zwingli accepted an appointment to Einsiedeln, about fifteen miles west of Glarus. Einsiedeln was Switzerland's major pilgrimage center. In 861 a monk named Saint Meinrad had been murdered there by two nobles; a Benedictine monastery was erected to commemorate this event. Miraculous healings soon were ascribed to the Black Madonna in the monastery chapel. Some claimed that the Virgin Mary had appeared there.

The inscription over the monastery entrance offered a plenary (full) indulgence to all who made a pilgrimage there. As a humanist priest, Zwingli found this difficult to accept. Although his income depended on the gifts pilgrims left at the monastery, he publicly questioned making pilgrimages for salvation's sake. "Christ alone saves, but he saves everywhere," he proclaimed. The number of pilgrims decreased, but the monastery's chief administrator, Diebold von Geroldseck, defended Zwingli and became a lifelong Zwingli supporter.[8] Zwingli later claimed that in 1516, before anyone had ever heard Luther's name mentioned, he had begun to preach the gospel at Einsiedeln.[9]

Despite Rome's misgivings about Zwingli's preaching, he still enjoyed the church's support for his propapal services and utterances. He used his pension to amass a fine library of more than three hundred volumes.[10] Zwingli's considerable leisure time at Einsiedeln afforded him opportunity to devour books from his own and the monastery's library. In addition to the classical historians and philosophers, the church fathers began to attract his attention.[11]

In 1518, Bernhardin Sanson, an unprincipled indulgence sales-man, began hawking his wares nearby. Zwingli attacked him, fully supported by Bishop Hugo of Constance in a letter written by the bishop's vicar, Johann Faber.[12] As a result, Sanson was recalled to Rome.

The Grossmünster in Zurich

Zwingli, the outspoken, scholarly priest, was gaining a reputation in German-speaking Switzerland. Others were interested in obtaining his leadership. Swiss Roman Catholicism stationed clergy by combin-ing a call system with episcopal approval. Zwingli rejected one such overture in 1517, but when a call came the next year to be priest at the Grossmünster ("Great Minster"), the principal church in Zurich, it piqued his interest. Oswald Myconius, Zwingli's humanist friend, had recommended him. Numerous Zurich pilgrims, who had heard Zwingli preach at Einsiedeln, enthusiastically endorsed the suggestion. The twenty-four canons (priests) attached to the Great Minster would have to make the decision, but the position appeared to be his.

A problem emerged, however. An honest man, Zwingli resisted moving to Zurich under false pretenses. He wrote a letter to an influential Great Minster canon confessing that while he had never committed adultery or dishonored a virgin or a nun, he had broken his vow of chastity at Glarus and had had an affair at Einsiedeln. He blamed only himself and confessed his weakness.[13] This candid admission did not injure Zwingli's chances. Clerical celibacy was not rigorously enforced in Switzerland at that time. Priests were allowed to pay fines for children they had fathered. Some paid the bishop an annual fee for the privilege of having housekeepers with whom they lived as husband and wife.[14] As well, Zwingli's chief contender for the Zurich position admitted that he and his concubine had six children.[15] In December of 1518 the canons, by a vote of seventeen to seven, elected Zwingli the "people's priest" at the Great Minster. The bishop approved.

Zwingli assumed his new position on January 1, 1519, his thirty-fifth birthday. John T. McNeill described him aptly: "The shepherd's son out of the Toggenburg was now in the prime of manhood, moderately tall and notably handsome, a personality at once vigorous and gracious; equipped with solid learning and accustomed to diligent study; an expert mighty in the scriptures and gifted with unusual oratorical powers."[16]

The new pastor's approach was revolutionary. He laid aside the lectionary texts in order to preach a series of sermons on the life of Christ based upon Matthew's Gospel. During the remainder of his life, Zwingli's preaching would be an explication of various Old and New Testament books. Without using a manuscript, he mixed deep scholarship with clarity and simplicity in his sermons. The Great Minster began to fill on Sundays. Zwingli's market-day sermons reached the country people. Although his voice was rather weak and his delivery rapid, Zwingli was a powerful preacher seeking to effect change in people's hearts. One person remarked that in hearing Zwingli preach, he felt as if he had been lifted up by the hair and suspended in space.[17]

Zwingli's success in preaching was due largely to his strong belief that the word of God had transforming power. He once wrote, "Truly, the Word of God has its course as certain as the Rhine; one may dam it up for a long time but never obstruct it."[18]

Spiritual Deepening

Zwingli apparently had no "tower discovery" such as Martin Luther experienced. A close brush with death, however, mightily affected him. The bubonic plague broke out in Zurich in August

1519. It eventually claimed twenty-five hundred of the city's six thousand inhabitants, including Zwingli's younger brother, Andrew. Away from Zurich when the plague struck, Zwingli hurried back to minister to the sick and dying. In September the courageous priest was himself stricken and nearly died. Upon his recovery, he wrote a twelve-verse plague hymn, which included these lines:

> My God My Lord!
> Healed by thy hand,
> Upon the earth
> Once more I stand.
>
> Let sin no more
> Rule over me;
> My mouth shall sing
> Alone to thee.[19]

A change had transpired in Zwingli's life. However, it may have come not only from his approaching death's door. In 1522 he wrote that about seven or eight years earlier, philosophy and theology had prevented him from devoting himself entirely to the scriptures. Eventually the Holy Spirit led him to set these things aside and "learn the doctrine of God direct from his own Word." As he asked God for light, the scriptures became clearer to him.[20]

Increasingly, Zwingli's preaching dealt with sin and redemption, the latter through Christ's atoning sacrifice. He attacked monasticism, purgatory, and the invocation of saints because they lacked biblical support. He also resumed his attack on the hiring of Swiss mercenary soldiers. This bore fruit when Zurich became the first Swiss canton to forbid the selling of its young men into the service of France or even into the service of the pope himself. Rome had been patient with

Zwingli until this point because it counted on Zurich's military support.[21] Zwingli in 1520 had already resigned his papal pension.

Zurich's political situation clarified the courage Zwingli required to establish his Reformation. Unlike Luther, who rejoiced in the protection of supportive princes, Zwingli in democratic Switzerland had to rely on the votes of Zurich's city council. Zurich, a commercial and manufacturing center, was really a city-state surrounded by a countryside containing sixty thousand inhabitants. The Zurich city council made all major decisions. Zwingli moved cautiously, therefore, in his attempt to reform his adopted city because all proposed changes required city council approval.

The Initial Break with Rome

The Reformation of Zurich began on Ash Wednesday in 1522 when Zwingli and some friends met for a meal at the home of the local printer, Christopher Froschauer. While the others broke the Lenten fast prohibiting the eating of meat, Zwingli approved but did not participate. Soon after, in a sermon entitled *Regarding the Choice and Freedom of Foods,* he contended that Christians were free to eat all foods but should not abuse themselves thereby. Since the Bible contained no valid fasting rule, to eat or not eat was a matter of free choice. To break the fasting rule was no sin.[22] Zwingli's position echoed Luther's claim that in Christ believers are free from laws of human devising.

July of that year brought two further developments. One dealt with the arrival of Francis Lambert, a former Franciscan monk who, in a friendly debate before selected persons, was convinced by Zwingli that Christians could pray directly to God without interceding with the saints. One person in attendance was the mayor of Zurich, Mark Roist, without whose help the Zurich Reformation may not have succeeded. Likewise, a large number of rural priests supported Zwingli.

The other event that escalated tension occurred on July 2 when Zwingli and ten other priests appealed by letter to the bishop of Constance requesting the abolition of clerical celibacy. They cited biblical support for marriage of clergy and lamented the large number of Swiss priests living in concubinage. Their request went unheeded.

That same year Zwingli secretly married Anna Reinhard Meyer, a beautiful widow from a good Zurich family. Zwingli had met her children at church. Because of Anna's involvement in litigation over her deceased husband's estate, she and Ulrich did not have a public wedding until April 2, 1524, three months after the birth of their first child.[23] Their marriage seems to have been a happy one. Three of the four children survived their father.

Zwingli's Early Publications

In August 1522, Zwingli's *Archeteles* came off the press. Published in Latin and later in German, it was Zwingli's denial that he taught heresy. He defended the biblical foundation on which he based his reforms, strongly suggesting that the Rock on which the church was built was Christ himself and not the papacy founded on Peter. A criticism of the church's wealth and worldliness followed. This book initiated Zwingli's keenly felt break with Erasmus.

Religious tension so mounted in Zurich that the city council determined that in early 1523 a public disputation be held to resolve matters. All discussion was to be conducted in German. The council invited the bishop of Constance, in whose diocese Zurich was located, to attend or send representatives. Clearly, not the church but the Zurich city council, after hearing the biblical interpretations of the theological experts, would make the final decision. One reason this was possible was that the Swiss Roman Catholic bishops were less powerful than bishops elsewhere.[24]

In order to clarify the issues for discussion at the forthcoming disputation, Zwingli published his *Sixty-Seven Conclusions.* It came out just before the gathering took place. The first fifteen conclusions focused on Christ as Savior. The second conclusion gave clear evidence of Zwingli's evangelical theology: "The sum and substance of the Gospel is that our Lord Jesus Christ, the true son of God, has made known to us the will of his heavenly Father, and has with his sinlessness released us from death and reconciled us to God."[25]

The theses immediately following designated Christ as the only way to salvation and stipulated that all who believed in him formulated his body on earth, of which he was the head. There was a certain bite in Zwingli's statements. For example, he contended that Christ was our only high priest (and those who have designated themselves high priests opposed Christ's honor and glory); Christ's death on the cross was for all eternity a sufficient sacrifice for the sins of all believers (and therefore it followed that the mass was not a sacrifice but a commemoration of Calvary); Christ was the only mediator between God and ourselves (clearly implying that no other intercession is necessary); and Christ was our only justification (and our works are good only if done in him).

The later theses decried the amassing of wealth in Christ's name, unbiblical restrictions laid on people (such as abstentions from foods and prohibition of marriage for clergy), excommunication performed by any other than the congregation of which the wrongdoer was a part, payment of fines to justify clerical concubinage, confession to priests for remission of sin, purgatory, and the notion that ordination conveyed an indelible character on a priest.[26]

The Disputations of 1523

Excitement prevailed when some six hundred people crowded into the Zurich city hall on the morning of January 29, 1523, for the debate regarding the Reformation already underway in Zurich. Among those representing the bishop was his vicar, Johann Faber, Zwingli's friend from their university days.

After opening statements by Mayor Roist and a representative of the bishop, Zwingli recalled how human-invented holiness and worship had dimmed the word of God in times past. He admitted being one of those who had recently been teaching that salvation was found in Jesus Christ alone and not in human works and merit. When he challenged those who considered his preaching and teaching heretical to speak their piece, no one responded.

Faber, calling Zwingli his good friend and brother, then affirmed that he too all these years had preached the gospel and now wished to hear those who allegedly opposed his interpretations. Again, silence reigned.[27]

Faber was outmaneuvered and outnumbered, however. He had first seen a copy of the *Sixty-Seven Conclusions* shortly before his arrival in Zurich, and he knew he was in "Zwingli country" when he told the gathering that only a general church council was competent to decide the issues before it. Failing that, universities such as Paris, Cologne, or Louvain could be consulted. Zwingli brought the house down by interrupting, "And why not Erfurt or Wittenberg?" When Faber later commented that for twelve hundred years priests had not been allowed to marry, a Zwingli supporter shouted, "But they have been allowed to take prostitutes."[28]

As the debate continued, it was clear that Roman Catholicism and Protestantism fundamentally differed on the issue of authority, the basis on which we formulate our beliefs. Faber, who held a doctorate in theology, defended "the praiseworthy institutions of the church" (fasting, festivals, the mass) as "something always decreed and ordered by the holy fathers." Zwingli, quoting Matthew 15:1-9 where our Lord asked the Pharisees why they had transgressed the commandment of God for the sake of their tradition, replied that the best way to honor God was "to obey his word, to live according to his will, not according to our ordinances and best opinion."[29] The two leaders' views pitted against one another Roman Catholicism's reliance on the church's tradition along with scripture in making theological judgments and Protestantism's dependence on scripture alone.

At the end of the afternoon session, the mayor and city council declared that since Zwingli was not convicted of heresy he should continue to proclaim "the Gospel and the pure sacred Scriptures" and that all priests in the canton should do the same.[30]

About nine hundred people attended a second Zurich disputation on October 26–28 that same year. This time the bishop and the Roman Catholic cantons did not send representatives. Zwingli and his supporters spent most of the time devising a strategy for the spread of Zwingli's Reformation. A key event at this session was Zwingli's sermon, *The Shepherd,* in which he contrasted good and counterfeit pastors. Good pastors' lives reflected Christlike fearlessness aroused by faith in the resurrection of Christ. "Not to fear is the armor," the reformer contended in one of his most famous statements.[31]

Zwingli's Reformation

Assured solid political support, the Swiss Reformation undertook significant changes. In June 1524 the city council effected the orderly removal by craftsmen of pictures and statuary in Zurich cantonal churches. They forbade pilgrimages. They diverted revenues that had previously supported the priests at the Great Minster to fund a theological school and a hospital for the poor. They closed the local monasteries, although they allowed their older members to depart with pensions.

On Maundy Thursday 1525, Zwingli's new liturgy, set in the Swiss-German dialect, replaced the Latin mass. Gone or soon to disappear were organ music, congregational singing, the eucharistic vestments, candles, and incense. Zwingli and other clergy spoke prayers antiphonally with brief responses uttered by the congregation. The men and women also spoke antiphonally the Gloria in Excelsis Deo and the Apostles' Creed. Zwingli and other clergy wore black academic gowns.

At the quarterly Lord's Supper services, Zwingli now stood behind a table in the nave facing the congregation. Wooden platters and goblets replaced the silver and gold mass vessels. Following the consecration prayer and Christ's Words of Institution, the clergy partook of the bread and wine, after which they served the congregation seated at tables in the nave. The laity received the cup as well as the bread. Following a prayer based on Psalm 113, Zwingli gave the benediction. All was performed in the greatest simplicity and clarity, which Zwingli so highly valued.[32]

Difficult to explain is Zwingli's rejection of the use of music in worship. Of the three major reformers, he was the most gifted musically. He had mastered almost every musical instrument of his time: the lute, harp, violin, pocket violin, cornet, and French horn.[33] The reformer offered little explanation, but since chant and choir songs were all in Latin and unintelligible for most laity, Zwingli silenced all liturgical music in 1527; all organs were either boarded up or removed.[34] Fortunately, music was restored to Zwinglian worship before the end of the sixteenth century.[35] However, simplicity with a strong emphasis on the spoken word still characterizes Swiss Reformed worship.

Translation of the Holy Scriptures

Like Luther, Zwingli came to the early conclusion that the scriptures needed to be translated so that priests and literate laypeople could read them. Beginning in July of 1525 all Zurich clergy and theological students began holding early morning, two-hour exegetical sessions in the Great Minster five days a week. Instructors read biblical texts in Latin, Greek, and Hebrew prior to a sermon based on these texts preached in German. Many laypersons came to hear the sermon. The whole procedure was called The Prophecy, a reference to 1 Corinthians 14 where Paul discussed prophecy as a telling forth of the word of God for the edification of the church.[36]

From these learned deliberations came the Zurich Bible of 1529.[37] In 1524 a Swiss-dialect version of Luther's New Testament had appeared in Zurich. The zeal of Zwingli and his Prophecy colleagues brought about the publication of the entire Bible in Swiss-German (even preceding the publication of the entire Luther Bible). Zwingli's desire that the Bible speak clearly to his fellow Swiss is apparent in his translation of the beginning of the Twenty-third Psalm: "The Lord is my shepherd. I shall not want. He makes me rest in lovely Alpine pastures."[38]

The Spread of Zwinglianism

The adherence of a number of former Roman Catholic priests, some of them originally Christian humanists like Zwingli, made possible the spread of Zwinglianism in Switzerland. Sebastian Hofmeister, a former Franciscan, evangelized the town of Schaffhausen. The intrepid efforts of Zwingli's friend Vadianus, a medical doctor and community leader, compelled the town of Saint Gall to join itself to Zwingli's Reformation. Capito (Wolfgang Koepfel) and Oecolampadius (Johann Hussgen) were the reformers of the town of Basel. Oecolampadius was an excellent biblical scholar, gifted in Hebrew and an assistant to Erasmus when the latter published his Greek New Testament. (Recall that at that time scholars used Latin versions of their last names.) These men began biblical preaching, German-language worship, and domination of the local publishing house, causing Erasmus in 1523 to complain, "They print everything favorable to Luther; nothing in favor of the Pope."[39]

Oecolampadius's friendship with Zwingli began in 1522. Four years later, when Johann Eck challenged Zwingli to debate and the latter reluctantly refused because he did not trust the proffered safe conduct to come to nearby Baden, Oecolampadius stood in for Zwingli. Although Oecolampadius was aided by notes from Zwingli smuggled into Baden almost daily by a young man disguised as a poultry dealer, Oecolampadius's quiet dignity and equally able scholarship represented the Protestant cause well. Yet Eck was declared the winner by an 87-12 vote. Eck had deftly depicted the growing differences between Luther and Zwingli, thus aiming to portray the uselessness of Protestantism's sole reliance on biblical authority.

The efforts of Berthold Haller won the town of Bern for Zwinglianism. After the 1527 election the city council was more reform-minded and sent out invitations to a 1528 disputation. Now it was Eck's turn to distrust a Protestant offer of safe conduct. This time Zwingli participated, as did Oecolampadius. It was clearly a Protestant victory. Conrad Troeger, an Augustinian monk and chief Roman Catholic spokesman, left early. He conceded to Zwingli's profound biblical knowledge, lamenting: "That beast is more learned than I thought."[40] An artist captured on canvas the account of a

Roman Catholic priest in his vestments waiting to say mass when Zwingli should conclude his January 18, 1528, sermon at Bern. So impressed was the priest that, laying his chasuble on the altar, he vowed to never say mass again.[41]

G. R. Potter appropriately designates the Bern disputation as the highest point of Zwingli's career. By convincing that large canton to embrace his Reformation, the reformer effected a triumphant reply to the Roman Catholic victory at Baden. Bern's becoming reformed helped prevent Zurich's isolation; it later served as support for Farel and Calvin's Reformation of Geneva; and it indirectly bolstered the Lutheran Reformation in Germany.[42]

Basel was not yet fully reformed, however. Several capable preachers of the old faith supported a strong pro-Roman Catholic faction. At Christmas of 1528, armed bands of Protestants and Roman Catholics walked the streets at night. By early January, however, it was clear that Oecolampadius's inspiring preaching was making a difference. When in February the conservative city council felt forced to accept the proposed reforms, Erasmus and a number of university faculty left in disgust.

Although Strassburg was technically an imperial city and not a part of Switzerland, its close ties to the Swiss Reformation require its inclusion here. The combined efforts of Matthew Zell, Martin Bucer, Capito, and the statesman Johann Sturm reformed this Rhineland city. Zell pioneered the reform work with his popular preaching in the cathedral. When the bishop forbade his further use of the stone pulpit, the carpenters' guild built a wooden one from which he preached to congregations numbering more than three thousand people.

Most of these reformers and a number of Strassburg priests married. In 1523 Matthew Zell married Katharine Schütz, who was an outstanding pastor's wife. She became known for her honest convictions, intelligent correspondence, and gracious hospitality. Strassburg was a city of Protestant refugees. Katharine Zell once had eighty people staying in their parsonage.[43] This intrepid woman contributed much to the Strassburg reformation long after her husband's death.

By 1524, Protestantism had a firm hold in Strassburg. That year Diebold Schwartz introduced a German liturgy in the cathedral. Johann Sturm was soon installed as rector of the Strassburg gymnasium, which provided an excellent educational foundation for reformation. Nonetheless, Martin Bucer emerged as the "soul of the church at Strassburg." He created the office of *kirchenpfleger* (church warden), which provided strong lay leadership for the church's self-discipline. He stressed congregational singing, revived confirmation, and pioneered in the creation of small disciple groups. Thanks to his efforts at reconciling Luther and Zwingli, as well as his participation in major Roman Catholic/Protestant reunion conversations, he gained a reputation as a "fanatic for unity."[44] His *Instruction in Christian Love* and *On the Kingdom of Christ* testify to the nobility and charity of his reform efforts.

The Swiss Religious Wars

The spread of Zwingli's Reformation exacerbated religious tensions in Switzerland. Zwingli realized his aim of seeing Zurich at the head of a political and military alliance when by 1529 the newly formed Christian Civic Union included Zurich, Bern, Basel, Constance, Schaffhausen, Biel, Saint Gall, and Mühlhausen in Alsace. Strassburg joined in 1530. The conservative high-Alpine and more rural cantons—Lucerne, Schwyz, Unterwalden, Zug, and Uri—formed in April 1529 the Roman Catholic Christian Alliance.

Friction mounted. The Protestants tried and beheaded Max Wehrli, an aggressive Roman Catholic official, for violence committed against their people. Sometime later, Jacob Kaiser, a fiery Zwinglian preacher, was arrested in jointly administered territory and on May 29, 1529, in Schwyz was burned at the stake for heresy. On June 8, Zurich declared war on the Christian Alliance.

Both sides put armies in the field. They met at Kappel, not far from Zurich. The Protestants numbered about thirty thousand, while the Roman Catholics had only some nine thousand poorly armed soldiers. The Swiss were reluctant to fight one another. Before hostilities could begin, the soldiers fraternized and the officers negotiated. The Christian Alliance troops produced a huge tub of milk and the Zurichers had bread enough and to spare. Soldiers from both sides mingled on the field together, satisfying hunger and thirst. The Christian Alliance leaders publicly tore up their secret treaty with Austria and promised to let people in the disputed territories decide their future religious affiliation by popular vote. Zwingli's demand that there be opportunity for reformed preaching throughout the Swiss Confederation was not adopted, however.

While it looked like a Protestant victory in that the Christian Alliance seemed to accept the permanence of the Reformed church in Switzerland, Zwingli was unhappy with the results. He believed that the Roman Catholics had made generous terms because of their numerical inferiority. Disgust permeates his oft-quoted remark: "For this peace which some are so strenuously pressing upon us means war, not peace. And the war upon which I am insisting is not war, but peace."[45]

The Marburg Colloquy

Zwingli had eagerly received Prince Philip of Hesse's April 1529 invitation to him and Martin Luther to meet for theological discussion. He hoped that this discussion would unite the two wings of the magisterial or state-supported Reformation against the papal forces.

Philip's timing was good. The Lutheran princes and free cities had just signed their *Protestatio* against the emperor. Zwingli hoped to strengthen his flagging political power by cooperating with the Lutherans. He promptly replied that he would attend.

For several years, Luther and Zwingli with their lieutenants had engaged in a literary war over the Lord's Supper. Zwingli had published *On the Lord's Supper* in 1526. Luther responded the next year with *That These Words of Christ "This Is My Body, etc." Still Stand Firm Against the Fanatics.* The sharply worded title of Luther's book typifies the deeply felt eucharistic struggle and promised plenty of theological fireworks whenever the two reformers would meet.

The theological colloquy was scheduled for early October 1529 at Prince Philip's castle at Marburg in Hesse. Zwingli kept his destination a closely guarded secret. Accompanied by two friends, he joined Oecolampadius and a colleague in Basel before sailing down the Rhine to Strassburg. Here they tarried for two weeks before traveling overland accompanied by Martin Bucer and others. Luther, Melanchthon, and three other theologians represented the Lutheran side.

At 6:00 A.M. on October 1, the discussions began. Philip wisely paired Luther and Oecolampadius in discussion in one room and Zwingli with Melanchthon in another. An early heated exchange between the volatile Luther and Zwingli would have ruined the conversations from the outset. Both morning and afternoon, these two sets of protagonists discussed the Lord's Supper. Oecolampadius later reported that Luther was as confrontational as Johann Eck; Zwingli found Melanchthon to be "uncommonly slippery."[46]

On October 2 at 6:00 A.M., the entire conference gathered in a large room (which is preserved intact to this day). Luther, the first speaker, uncovered the words *"Hoc est corpus meum"* ("This is my body"), which he had earlier written in chalk on the table. He insisted that he would hold to this literal interpretation despite the more rational arguments he expected from the Swiss and Southwest Germans. Oecolampadius replied that he and his colleagues were also biblical, but that the Bible was replete with metaphors (words applied to an object that are not to be taken literally but to suggest another meaning). The phrase "This is my body" was one of these. He then quoted John 6:63, "It is the spirit that gives life; the flesh is useless," a verse strongly supporting a spiritual rather than a real reception of Christ's body and blood. Zwingli entered the fray attacking Luther's idea that Christians must actually eat Christ's body and blood.

Zwingli prefaced his remarks by expressing his delight at meeting Luther and Melanchthon. Luther replied that he too wanted peace between the two Protestant groups, but he would not budge on his literal interpretation of "This is my body." Neither side yielded as the debate continued on October 3.

The differences between Luther and Zwingli regarding their interpretations of the Lord's Supper emerge partially out of their theological training and professional backgrounds. Luther, who spent thirteen years in an Augustinian monastery, had been schooled at Erfurt University by faculty members who minimized the role of reason in making faith judgments. He was also more mystically inclined. He could easily interpret our Lord's words spoken over the bread and wine at the Last Supper in a literal sense. For him Christ's body and blood were really present in, with, and under the bread and wine. Depending upon Colossians 1:15 and following he believed that the resurrected Lord was everywhere present and was available to the eyes of faith in the bread and wine when the word—the gospel—was spoken over them. He encouraged his followers to receive the Lord's Supper frequently, citing Christ's words in Matthew 26 that it was for the forgiveness of sin.

Zwingli was more rational both by nature and by training. He had studied under professors who stressed the cooperation of faith and reason in the search for theological truth. He was a parish priest and not a monk. For him the figurative interpretation of Christ's words made much more sense. If the body of Christ was in heaven (as the Apostles' Creed affirmed), then it could not be really present in the bread and wine. Zwingli felt content that his people receive the Lord's Supper four times a year. He taught them that it was a eucharist (a thanksgiving) in which by coming forward and receiving the Supper around a table in the chancel, they testified to their faith.

Because scholars referred to Luther's teaching to imply Christ's "Real Presence" in the Lord's Supper, others (irreverently and not totally accurately) refer to Zwingli's teaching as connoting Christ's "Real Absence."

Toward the end of the disputation, Luther composed fourteen articles affirming basic Christian doctrines such as the Trinity, the Incarnation, the unity of Christ's two natures, original sin, redemption through faith in Christ's atonement, and several that repudiated practices of the medieval church. Others of these insisted on Communion in both kinds for the laity but confessed disagreement on Christ's physical presence in the bread and wine of the Lord's Supper. All the participants signed these articles. Despite expressions of Christian charity as far as was compatible with conscience and mutually promised prayers for the Holy Spirit's guidance, the Marburg Colloquy adjourned, failing to achieve Philip of Hesse and Zwingli's cherished hopes of political and military union.

Zwingli's Death

Upon his return from Marburg, Zwingli continued his political endeavors on behalf of the Reformation. Confident in the power of the preached word to draw people to his evangelical sermons, he persuaded Zurich to demand unhindered Reformed preaching throughout Switzerland. Ironically, at the same time, the Roman Catholic mass was forbidden in all the Reformed cantons because it was deemed in opposition to the Bible.[47]

In April and May of 1531, representatives of the Swiss Protestant cities discussed how to open the Catholic cantons to Reformed preaching. Bern opposed war and favored an embargo on grain, meat, salt, iron, and other necessities the Catholic cantons did not produce. Zwingli opposed this for the hardship it would work on women and children. To him, military force was preferable. The blockade failed. It also heightened Roman Catholic hostility. Zwingli's disappointments mounted. Bern proved to be an indecisive ally and the Zurich authorities made inadequate military preparation, despite intelligence that the Christian Alliance was mobilizing its forces.

On October 11, 1531, the eight-thousand-man Roman Catholic army encountered the hastily marshaled Protestant force numbering fifteen hundred soldiers once again at Kappel. This time there was no negotiation. In the late afternoon battle, five hundred Zurich men (including twenty-five Reformed clergymen) died, as well as about one hundred Roman Catholics. That day the grieving Anna Zwingli lost her husband, son, brother, brother-in-law, and son-in-law.

Zwingli in battle wore a steel helmet and carried both a sword and battle axe. When severely wounded, he refused the victor's offer to receive last rites. By torchlight, an officer recognized him and delivered the sword thrust that brought instant death. Reportedly, just before dying Zwingli uttered Socrates' words, "They can destroy the body but not the soul."[48]

A priest with the victorious army bent over the reformer's lifeless body and with tears declared, "Whatever you may have been by reason of your faith, I know that you were an honest Confederate."[49] Over the objection of some of their officers, the victorious Christian Alliance soldiers quartered Zwingli's body, smeared it with manure, and burned it. Zwingli's friend Myconius reported that three days later when the reformer's friends visited the battlefield seeking traces of him, they found his heart lying whole and undamaged in the ashes.[50]

The Second Peace of Kappel guaranteed Zurich's independence but forced it to surrender all its alliances. Each canton would decide by majority vote to be Roman Catholic or Reformed, but the latter would have no minority rights in Catholic cantons. Reformed preaching in the jointly administered territories was abolished. Increasing the Reformed gloom was the news that on November 21 Oecolampadius had died. A frail man, the news of Zwingli's death was apparently too much for him.

Heinrich Bullinger

Fortunately, new and able Reformed leadership arose when the Zurich city council chose Heinrich Bullinger (1504–75) to serve as Zwingli's successor. Son of a Roman Catholic priest who had also opposed indulgences, Bullinger had studied at Cologne University. Reading the New Testament, Luther, and Melanchthon caused his conversion to Protestantism in 1522. In 1528 he married Anna Adlischweiler, a former nun, who greatly enhanced his ministry. Besides caring for their eleven children, she made provision in later years for the large number of Protestant refugees seeking asylum in Zurich.

On December 9, 1531, at age twenty-seven, Bullinger mounted the pulpit of the Great Minster. His sermon was like a *sursum corda* ("Lift up your hearts") to the saddened congregation. On hearing Bullinger preach, people thought that Zwingli was not dead or that, like the phoenix, he had been restored to life.

Bullinger was just what the unsettled Zurich situation needed. Described as talented, wise, firm, and compassionate,[51] he was also an able theologian who published in 1534 *The One and Eternal Testament or Covenant of God.* In this he traced God's one covenant in history initiated with Adam and Eve and renewed with Noah, Abraham, Moses, David, and Christ. Through this everlasting agreement, God promised to be all-sufficient to those who keep the covenant conditions through faith in God through Christ, pious living, and love of neighbor. Covenant theology was central to Bullinger's thought in his forty-four-year leadership of the Swiss Reformation.[52] He used the Old Testament community to serve as the model for the Christian church. As a result, circumcision as entrance rite into the Old Testament community was succeeded by infant baptism in the church. Christian pastors, like the Old Testament prophets, were to use the word to urge people to keep God's covenant. Christian magistrates were to emulate Old Testament kings whose task it was to establish religion and discipline the people.

Bullinger's widespread influence was due first to the vast number of religious refugees that came to Zurich. A number of English clergymen drew upon his ideas in later reforming the church in their native land. Second, Bullinger maintained a voluminous correspondence. It appears that he wrote almost twelve thousand letters, almost three times that of Luther or Calvin.[53] His lack of personal ambition and graciousness caused many persons to seek his wise counsel.

Bullinger's third major contribution lay in his publications. He was largely responsible for drawing up in 1536 the First Helvetic (Swiss) Confession. In 1549 he and Calvin labored together to author the *Consensus Tigurinus* (*Tigurinus* was the Latin name for Zurich) by which the German- and French-speaking Reformed churches drew much closer to one another. His Second Helvetic Confession of 1566 was adopted by the Reformed churches in his own and other European countries. Bullinger's *Decades* (fifty sermons), published in 1549, became popular reading in Reformed circles. Blessed with a more congenial nature and a long life, Bullinger successfully built on the foundation Zwingli had laid.

ZWINGLI'S UNDERSTANDING OF THE CHRISTIAN FAITH

The preceding pages clearly illustrate how Zwingli's beliefs motivated his reformatory actions. They also remind us that a major reason Zwingli published less than Luther or Calvin was his untimely death, which cut short the productivity of his pen. Nevertheless, his published writings evidence his strong faith.

In 1522, Zwingli's sermons to the Dominican nuns in Zurich were published under the title *Of the Clarity and Certainty of the Word of God.* He insisted that human beings, created in the divine image, have a particular longing for God. Nothing will delight them more than the word of God, which is God's speech whereby creation happens and redemption is promised. It is alive and strong.[54] The Word is the Son of God, who was incarnated in the Virgin Mary. The gospel preached and taught about this divine/human encounter is now an accomplished fact.[55] It is the good news that God gives to ignorant and doubtful people.[56] Twice in this treatise the reformer quoted Peter's poignant response in John 6:68 to our Lord's question whether the apostles would also abandon him, saying, "Lord, to whom can we go? You have the words of eternal life."[57] The power in God's word is that it draws us to God. Such confidence made Zwingli a bold preacher and activist.

Zwingli's *Commentary on True and False Religion* was published in 1525. William Farel, later Calvin's fellow reformer in Geneva, persuaded him to write it in order to convince the French king, Francis I.[58] Written in Latin, this three-hundred-page book became Zwingli's major theological work. The essence of true religion, he contended, was based on the word of God. God remains inaccessible to human reason and must be known by self-revelation. Religion took its rise when God, seeking runaway humanity, called out in the Garden of Eden, "Adam, where are you?" Religion is grounded in the loyal devotion of God to sinful humanity in bountiful grace that calls the wanderer home. When people utterly despair of themselves, they respond in faith to this grace. Zwingli offered a classic definition of faith: "This clinging to God, therefore, with an unshaken trust in Him as the only good, as the only one who has the knowledge and the power to relieve our troubles and to turn away all evils or to turn them to His own glory and the benefit of His people, and with filial dependence on Him as a father—this is piety, is religion."[59] False religion, by contrast, is trusting anything other than God.

All of this reveals Zwingli's pessimistic view of humanity. Piety is born when persons realize that, on their own, they have no means of pleasing God, who abounds in so much love that persons in the divine care lack nothing. Scripture abundantly confirms this. Indeed, "all the pious really sing no other song than that we have nothing, God lacks nothing, by Him nothing is denied."[60] This meager estimation of human ability stems from Zwingli's doctrine of sin. It is a disease causing us to despair of our righteousness and salvation; it is like a mortal wound. Consequently, for the rest of our lives true and continued repentance is necessary as we rely upon God's forgiving grace.[61] Zwingli's identification with Augustine's dour description of the human condition is clear in the comment penned in the margin of his own copy of *The City of God:* "Ah, God, if only Adam had eaten a pear!"[62]

Zwingli affirmed the doctrine of God's providence. Once while walking in the woods and watching a squirrel ferry itself across a stream on a piece of wood, he saw in this event marvelous evidence for the divine providence that gives even dumb animals the intelligence needed for their existence. God is the first cause and highest good of all that exists. It made no sense to suggest that God created the universe only to let it govern itself.

This belief carried over into salvation. Predestination depended on providence, its mother. In salvation, people do not elect God; God elects them. Faith precedes from election, not vice versa. Those will be saved to whom God gives the faith to receive salvation; all others will be damned.

Zwingli carried these doctrines out to radical conclusion, but without the logical consistency Calvin would later give them. Still, the Zurich reformer "bit the bullet," admitting that if God directed all things, God was the author of evil. He also believed that Socrates and other classical pagan authors would be saved without belief in Christ because God was free to choose whomever God would.[63]

In his *Commentary on True and False Religion,* Zwingli staked out his ground regarding the sacraments, which were nothing more than initiation rites or ceremonials by which people made pledges to God. They had no cleansing power, and the Holy Spirit was not bound to act in and through them.[64] In his 1525 treatise *Of Baptism* he preferred the inward baptism of the Holy Spirit to water baptism. Still, the latter was important because it was a covenant sign of initiation into Christ, just as circumcision was an Old Testament covenant sign.[65]

In 1526 Zwingli published *On the Lord's Supper,* in which he contended that since sacraments were signs of holy things, the sign and the thing signified could not be one and the same. Thus, the sacrament of Christ's body and blood was not the same as the body and blood itself.[66]

Like Luther, Ulrich Zwingli offers suggestions for living the Christian life in our time. One of these suggestions stressed the otherness of God, a belief not wholly acceptable to many late-twentieth-century Christians. Like Luther, Zwingli depicted God's mystery by invoking Isaiah's statement: "Truly, you are a God who hides himself" (Isa. 45:15). The Swiss reformer contended that we know as little about God as a beetle does about a man. Indeed, God is much farther from humanity than humanity is from a beetle.[67]

This divine inaccessibility makes God's self-revelation all the more significant. Even the best human minds cannot know God on their own. To be sure, God created human beings in God's image and, as such, they thirst after the divine presence and long for eternal life. They are conscious of their basic yearning to be united with the God who gave them breath.[68] Such longing, said Zwingli, is not sufficient to unite us with God, however.

It was natural then for Zwingli to fasten upon Adam as a runaway man who hid himself in his anguish, only to be pursued by a merciful God who asked him where he was, "Adam, where are you?" God, knowing where Adam in his misery was located, still gently asked the question in order to remind our first parent of the sad state into which he had fallen. For Zwingli this adequately proved that God, transcendent and far beyond human grasp, was nonetheless "a strong lover of souls."[69] If religion consists of pious devotion, it is obviously founded upon the father's loyal devotion to his undutiful son. Zwingli acknowledged that the matter goes both ways: True religion involves humanity's loyal devotion to God as well. "But pious devotion is complete only when we turn to the one who calls us away from ourselves and our designs."[70] Zwingli had it right. The gospel is never about our searching for God; it is always the good news that God is searching for us. People mean well when they say, "I have found the Lord." It would be much truer to biblical doctrine and, in all likelihood to their experience, for them to affirm that the Lord had found them.

Second, Zwingli's assessment of our human condition offers valuable insights. He rightfully noted that self-seeking led our first parents to fall away from God, and this misplaced affection continues to cause problems today.[71]

Zwingli was confident that our focus upon ourselves and upon that which we think will bring us gratification keeps us from trusting God's promises in Christ for our redemption. Because we do not trust what God has done and is doing for our salvation, we get caught up in trying to resolve our alienation from God by doing good works. These, we think, will meet the divine expectations. How ironic that we should offer God good works when God, at this point, expects only faith from us. By seeking to set things right through our own action we are saying, in effect, that we would rather depend upon our own works than rely on God's grace; that we would rather rely on ourselves than trust God. Zwingli here used the Apostle Paul's somber warning: "For whatever does not proceed from faith is sin" (Rom. 14:23).[72] Thus, "the sin above all sins is unbelief."[73]

Complicating this picture of humanity was Zwingli's reminder that God expects perfect righteousness of human beings! Unfortunately, they cannot produce it. The devastating result of our sad inheritance of Adam and Eve's sinful condition is that we totally lack the ability to justify ourselves before God. Somewhat sympathetically and yet quite realistically Zwingli summarized our plight by saying that "we are set between the hammer and the anvil, half beast and half angel."[74]

Many people today object to this sober view of humankind.

They contend that it discourages people from seeking to live a Christian life, from believing the best about their neighbors, and from trying to make the world a better place in which to live. Such pessimism, they argue, continues to serve oppressors in their domination of the oppressed. Persons of greater optimism predict a better and brighter world if each person is allowed to live up to his or her God-given potential.

Zwingli would not agree, even though he was aware of the complexity of social and personal problems people faced in his much simpler age. Were he alive today he would only need to point out that the twentieth century, labeled "the Christian century" by optimistic Christians around 1900, has been the bloodiest hundred-year period in recorded history. Its cruel repressions were even committed by people well educated in the sciences that offered to elevate humanity to better standards of living and greater avenues of achievement and independence. Zwingli's observation of daily existence as he knew it and his reading of holy scripture conspired to raise his sensitivity to humanity's inability to extricate itself from its serious problems, and this offers a third insight for modern living. People should not be flattered into thinking they have virtues and abilities that they do not possess. Zwingli's solution for all people was to "go down into themselves" in order to investigate all their concealments, pretenses, and dissimulations.[75] Such honest self-examination drives us to despair about what we can do for ourselves. Only then can we become open to the divine grace that can call, redeem, and save us. The "bad news" that makes us aware of our condition is the prerequisite for our receiving the "good news" that is God's grace.

Fourth, Zwingli's dour assessment of humankind caused heavy dependence upon divine assistance. He unashamedly relied on, and believed that nothing can bring greater delight to the inward person, than the word of God.[76] Like his reforming colleagues, Luther and Calvin, Zwingli stated how God's redemptive message addresses us in three ways: through Jesus Christ (John 1:1-18), through the preaching of the gospel, and through holy scripture. Each of these could appropriately be termed the word of God.

Of course, these three are interrelated. Jesus Christ is the Word made flesh. The preaching, teaching, and witnessing done in his name are also God's word. Another term for it is *the gospel.* The account of our Lord's teaching, life, death, and resurrection contained in holy scripture (as well as the Old Testament) is also designated the word of God.[77]

The biblical account of the Tower of Babel (Gen. 11) perfectly illustrates the need for a clear and redemptive word for the human race. The pride that led people to attempt building a tower that would reach the heavens caused God to disrupt their plans by confusing their languages. The resultant upheaval never saw a solution until Pentecost (Acts 2) when, in response to the miracle of the outpouring of the Holy Spirit, the opposite effect occurred. People of various nations heard the same gospel (word) each in his or her own language.

A cacophony of superficial appeals to feel, do, or buy something that promises gratification and well-being saturates our times. The human temptation to elevate ourselves into God's precincts, to which the people of Babel yielded, is alive and well today. It is reassuring to know that in the resultant chaos we create, God's word, spoken or read, still has power to call us out of our alienations, confusions, and miseries. Pentecost, with its offer of salvation and unity, is always ready to happen. Zwingli illustrated this with his contention: "If you think there can be no assurance or certainty for the soul, listen to the certainty of the Word of God."[78]

A last contribution to our discipleship from Zwingli's thought and action is his belief that the new life in Christ is an active one. He wrote to his stepson, Gerold Meyer: "For only believers know and experience the fact that Christ will not let his people be idle. They alone know how joyful and pleasant a thing it is to engage in his service."[79] Zwingli believed that faith causes people to do good works on behalf of others. We are not born to live for ourselves but to serve others even when it costs us something.[80] A Christian is one who does not merely speak about the laws of God but is "the one who with God's help attempts great things."[81]

We glimpse here Zwingli's courageous attempt at reforming the Swiss church, as well as his concern for those he felt the church and state were overlooking or oppressing in his time. He is one who "provides a model of vigorous Christian political involvement."[82] Zwingli was not given to heroism, nor did he joyfully seek the excitement of combat. For him, to live in Christ was to know freedom from the number-one sin, self-concern. He expected that persons so liberated could now give themselves actively on behalf of others.

Like most Christian leaders, Zwingli did not always live according to his teachings. His zeal for reform made him intolerant of his Roman Catholic counterparts (who were no less critical of him). It led him to take drastic measures against left-wing Protestants (who looked with dismay at his moderate Reformation). His driving activism caused his overinvolvement in political and military measures with which he sought to secure his Reformation. Zwingli combined within himself the strengths and flaws that constitute our common humanity.

In Zurich, next to the Water Church and near his beloved Great Minster, is a statue of Ulrich Zwingli. It depicts the reformer facing southward in the direction of the Roman Catholic cantons, which were his stalwart opponents. His determination is evident in his strong, set jaw and serene facial expression. In his right hand Zwingli clutches the holy scriptures; his left hand grasps the hilt of his sword. If we rightfully shrink back from Zwingli's attempt to spread the gospel by bloodshed, we can still gratefully acknowledge the passionate commitment and courageous leadership he offered because of his trust in God. We remember his guiding principle: "Not to fear is the armor." He also inspires those who come after him to attempt "something bold for God's sake."[83]

A PRAYER OF ULRICH ZWINGLI

Almighty, eternal and merciful God, whose Word is a lamp unto our feet and a light unto our path, open and illuminate our minds, that we may purely and perfectly understand thy Word and that our lives may be conformed to what we have rightly understood, that in nothing we may be displeasing unto thy majesty, through Jesus Christ our Lord. Amen.[84]

FOR PERSONAL OR GROUP REFLECTION

1. What aspects of Zwingli's life story do you find most significant?

2. Had you been a Zurich citizen in the early 1520s, would you have supported Zwingli's Reformation attempts in that canton? Why or why not?

3. One of Zwingli's well-remembered sayings is "Not to fear is the armor." State how you would apply this statement to your life of faith as you enter the twenty-first century.

4. Zwingli described faith in terms of one's "clinging to God" as the only good. How do you define faith?

5. Do you agree with Zwingli's contention that "we have nothing, God lacks nothing and by Him nothing is denied"? How does this relate to your understanding of prayer?

6. Where in your Christian experience do you recall that God came searching for you?

7. The Apostle Paul and Zwingli believed that the greatest sin is unbelief. Can you relate to that from your background?

8. Zwingli encouraged people to "go down into themselves" in honest self-examination. Is this encouraged too much or too little in our time? How has this self-examination proved valuable in your Christian life?

9. In what ways is Zwingli a good example of someone doing "something bold for God's sake"? How have you experienced God's call to do something bold for your faith?

10. Imagine you had been present at the Marburg Colloquy in 1529 where Martin Luther, Ulrich Zwingli, and their associates debated the meaning of the Lord's Supper. Which position would you have supported: Zwingli in his contention that the bread and wine are signs of Christ's body and blood or Luther who said that Christ's body and blood are in, with, and under the bread and wine?

JOHN
CALVIN

CHAPTER 3

"We Are Not Our Own But God's"

THE LIFE AND MINISTRY OF JOHN CALVIN

Georgia Harkness declared that of all the powerful figures of the sixteenth century, none left a more lasting heritage than John Calvin.[1] People who exercise such influence are usually not regarded indifferently; a historian described Calvin as "one of those strong and consistent men of history whom people liked or disliked, adored or abhorred."[2] Calvin's successor, Theodore Beza, honored the reformer and said of his death on May 27, 1564: "On that day, with the setting sun, the brightest light that was in the world for the guidance of God's church, was taken back to heaven."[3] Yet a twentieth-century biographer admitted that two things made Calvin terrible: his bad temper and his concept of predestination![4] Such comment constitutes an invitation to review Calvin's life and his ministry.

THE LIFE STORY OF JOHN CALVIN

John Calvin was born Jehan Cauvin on July 10, 1509, in Noyon, an episcopal city in the French province of Picardy. He would become a second-generation reformer. When Calvin was in the cradle, Luther was already a university professor and Zwingli a pastor.

The parental home into which the future reformer was born represented upward social mobility. Calvin's father, Gerard Cauvin, had departed his family's boatman trade to become a notary serving both priests and magistrates, as well as a secretary to the bishop of Noyon. His wife, Jeanne Lefranc Cauvin, was a woman of beauty and piety who died when little Jehan was three years old. As the boy grew, his father recognized the gifts of his precocious son and arranged to have several cathedral chaplaincies assigned to him even though he was just a minor.

With this financial aid, and in company with the sons of Noyon aristocrats, Jehan Cauvin entered Paris University in 1523 where, following custom, he latinized his name to Johannes Calvinus, the English version of which is John Calvin. At the College de la Marche, Calvin learned his excellent literary style under Mathurin Cordier, France's best Latin teacher. Later, Noel Beda, a sternly orthodox theologian at the College Montaigu, introduced Calvin to the subtleties of paradoxical thinking.

Erasmus, who had earlier studied at Montaigu, complained about the college's bad eggs and equally stale theology. It is unlikely that Calvin's later poor digestion resulted from bad refectory food but more possibly from his nervous nature and diligent study habits. His encyclopedic memory, sharp analytical capacity, and self-discipline made him an excellent student. His maturity even as a youth never permitted indulgence in the gaieties of university life, for which he occasionally censured his playful fellow students. They, in turn, called him "the accusative case"! Still, Calvin had a number of close friends, some of them the sons of Paris university professors. In 1528 he received his master's degree.

Calvin had been moving toward the priesthood, but his father's disfavor with the Noyon cathedral chapter and eventual excommunication caused the latter to insist that his son study law instead of theology. Calvin obediently entered the Orleans University law school. While he did not like legal studies, he applied himself with customary diligence. There Melchior Wolmar, a German professor, taught Calvin Greek. Like Cordier, his Latin teacher, Wolmar became Calvin's lifelong friend. Calvin was now a dedicated humanist, devoted to studying the languages and literature of antiquity. Although his father's death in 1531 would have freed him to forsake law and devote himself to the classics, he finished the course and sometime before January 1532 received his doctor of jurisprudence degree.

About this time, Calvin, who had published his commentary on Seneca in 1531, underwent his "sudden conversion." Perhaps the two leading direct influences on him in this regard were Wolmar, a convinced Lutheran, and Pierre Robert, Calvin's cousin from Noyon, who bore the nickname "Olivetan" because he "burned the midnight oil" pursuing his studies. By the late 1520s, Olivetan was a dedicated Protestant.

Calvin, sometimes described as one "difficult to know,"[5] was reluctant to share much autobiographical material. Scholars date his conversion somewhere between early 1530 and early 1534. Calvin's conversion was not from wickedness to piety or from doubt to belief, but rather from Roman Catholicism to evangelical faith. His restrained and poetic account of it appears in his 1557 *Commentary on the Psalms:*

> And first, since I was
> So obstinately devoted
> To the superstitions of the Papacy
> That it was difficult to pull me

Out of that very deep morass—
By a sudden conversion
God tamed and brought to teachableness
My heart, which, despite my youth,
Was too hardened in such matters.
Having therefore received
Some taste and knowledge
Of true piety,
I was suddenly fired
With such a great desire to advance
That, even though I had not forsaken
the other studies entirely,
I nonetheless worked at them
More slackly.[6]

Although Calvin described his conversion experience in intellectual terms one might expect an academic to use, we should not regard it as a mere enlightenment of the mind or a dedication of the will; a passion was at work. When Calvin later designed a seal for himself, he used a flaming heart standing erect on the palm of an outstretched hand with the accompanying words: "My heart I give thee, Lord, eagerly and entirely."[7] Calvin had appropriated God's grace emotionally as well as intellectually.

The young scholar had already turned activist. On November 1, 1533, his friend, Nicholas Cop, rector of the University of Paris, gave an address which, though not antipapal, attacked the church leaders of the day, using ideas that could have been borrowed from Erasmus and Luther. As a result, the theological faculty of the university cited both Cop and Calvin (the suspected author of the address) for heresy. The two friends fled Paris (Calvin disguised as a vinedresser), and

Calvin spent the year 1534 on the move. That year he formally broke with Rome by resigning all the church offices from which he was receiving financial support.

During his stay in Basel, Switzerland, in 1535–36, Calvin published his most famous work, *The Institutes of the Christian Religion.* He wrote in defense of the Protestants, whom the French king was arresting and killing. When the book first appeared in Basel in March 1536, it consisted of six chapters spread over 532 pages. Although Calvin wrote it in Latin and intended it for intellectuals, it surprisingly sold out in less than a year. Calvin continued to amend and enlarge the *Institutes,* translating them also into French. His last edition (1559 in Latin and 1560 in French) comprised four books, divided into seventy-nine chapters and filling 1,521 pages! Calvin looked upon his book as a key to open a way for all God's children to understand scripture correctly.[8]

First Geneva Ministry

The twenty-seven-year-old author was not in Basel when the *Institutes* first came off the press. Instead, he was for a short time in Italy and then France to settle his father's estate. Accompanied by his brother, Antoine, and his half-sister, Marie, he then departed for Strassburg. War conditions blocked the direct route, so the party detoured by way of Geneva, stopping there only for the night. In Geneva, William Farel, the red-bearded, fiery preacher who had introduced Protestantism to French-speaking Switzerland, accosted Calvin. Calvin refused Farel's request that he stay to help with the reformation of Geneva, pleading his desire to live a scholar's life. Farel's retort was that should Calvin refuse to help in the face of such urgent necessity, God would curse his scholarship. The little preacher's thunderous voice and confident manner so overwhelmed Calvin that he agreed to stay.

Some years later he wrote, "God has never let me rest in any place whatever, but in spite of my natural disposition, He has brought me forth into the light, and…has thrust me onto the stage."[9]

Geneva was then a frontier city situated between France, the other Swiss cantons, and the territories ruled by the dukes of Savoy. The ten thousand inhabitants crowded into its fortress walls dealt mainly in commerce. The local bishop had for years governed Geneva, supported by the duke of Savoy. The duke's efforts in 1519 to get "John the Bastard," the illegitimate son of a former bishop, appointed as episcopal leader occasioned the opposition party's attempt to overthrow episcopal rule. These unsuccessful rebels called themselves the Eidgenots, the possible origin of the term *Huguenots,* thereafter used to designate French Calvinists.

Farel, Pierre Viret, and other Protestant preachers capitalized on this anti-episcopal sentiment when they attempted reform of Geneva in the early 1530s. By August 1535, Farel's powerful preaching had overcome earlier reverses, and the city council abolished the mass. The departure of the Roman Catholic clergy enabled Farel to introduce Protestant worship. The situation was still fluid, and to Farel's credit he recognized in young Calvin the leadership the situation demanded.

Calvin, given the title "professor of sacred letters," began lecturing on Paul's epistles and joined the company of pastors although, interestingly, no evidence of his ordination survives. He published a catechism and *Instruction in Faith* for lay readers. Calvin's articles on worship called for frequent celebration of the Lord's Supper and supported the church's right to excommunicate those who did not so live that they could come to the Lord's table without profaning the sacrament. The city council reluctantly agreed to divide Geneva into twenty-six wards with lay officials appointed to report the names of those whose lives appeared unrepentant and disorderly.

The elections in January 1538 resulted in a new council unfavorable to Farel and to Calvin, who had come to be known as "that Frenchman." Matters worsened and on April 23, 1538, Calvin, Farel, and Elie Corauld, their blind colleague, were given three days in which to leave. The Geneva Reform had failed.

Calvin's Strassburg Ministry

Other clergy continued the Protestant ministry in Geneva. Farel accepted a church in Neuchatel; Corauld died; and Calvin finished his interrupted journey to Strassburg. Upon his arrival in the German-speaking city on the Rhine, its major reformer, Martin Bucer, urged him to answer the call to serve the French refugee congregation. With the Geneva failure fresh in mind, Calvin declined, pleading a preference for scholarship. Bucer "pulled a Farel" on Calvin, telling him it was God's will that he minister to this congregation and threatening him with God's ability to find a rebellious servant just as God found the runaway Jonah. Calvin heeded.

Calvin's three years pastoring this French congregation were the happiest of his life for several reasons. Martin Bucer was a powerful influence on Calvin; Bucer invited Calvin's attendance at a number of ecumenical conferences with Roman Catholic and Lutheran scholars. Calvin thereby forged a lifelong friendship with Philip Melanchthon, Luther's friend and successor. Calvin also gained great liturgical and pastoral experience. His congregation was known as a "singing church." The arrival of his old friend Clement Marot, who was busy translating the Psalms into French verse for singing purposes, enhanced Calvin's worship revisions. In 1542, Calvin published the first *Geneva Psalter* which, filled with Marot's versified psalms often set to music by Louis Bourgeois, would become a foundation for Calvinist worship in many languages.

Nor did Calvin's academic gifts lie idle in Strassburg. He lectured in theology in the academy founded by the outstanding educator, Johann Sturm. He also found time to publish his treatise on the Lord's Supper, his commentary on Romans, and one of his greatest literary pieces, the *Reply to Sadoleto.* Jacopo Sadoleto, an able and exemplary Roman Catholic archbishop, had written an enticing letter to the Genevans inviting their return to Roman Catholicism. Calvin's skillful letter clearly outlined the differences that existed between Protestantism and Rome, defending the former as an attempt to reform the true church. Calvin's respectful language and eloquent literary style characterize this masterpiece.

A final reason that the Strassburg years were Calvin's happiest was that he found a wife there. He had begun to think about marriage, though in 1539 he wrote Farel that he was not one of those "insane lovers" who get "smitten at first sight with a fine figure." The beauty he desired in a woman was that of good character, an obliging spirit, not hard to please, economical, and interested in caring for his health.[10]

Given these high standards it is amazing that Calvin's friends offered any matrimonial suggestions. The first was a wealthy German woman who did not speak French and gave no indication of learning the language; another was French and a devout Protestant, but fifteen years Calvin's senior; still another spoke French, but had no money. Calvin interviewed the last one, but nothing resulted. Then the reformer himself found a wife in his own congregation,[11] Idelette de Bure Stordeur, a widow. Her husband, Jean Stordeur, a Belgian artisan, was an Anabaptist leader. The Anabaptists were people who had broken away from Zwingli's reformation in Zurich because they had a more radical view of the faith. The Stordeurs later converted to Calvin's persuasion and were attending his Strassburg congregation when Jean Stordeur died of the plague in 1540, leaving Idelette and two children. Idelette was described as a cultured, honest, upright, and pretty woman. Calvin, always with "an eye for class," married her in 1541. Her son remained in Strassburg; her daughter lived with them in Geneva.

No children survived the Calvin marriage. A son, Jacques, was born prematurely and died in 1542. Idelette's health worsened, and she died in 1549. Calvin, unlike Luther, reported little about his home life. Testimony to the marital happiness he enjoyed, however, is apparent in his 1549 letter to Viret describing Idelette's death: "I have been bereaved of the best companion of my life, of one who, had it been so ordered, would not only have been the willing sharer of my indigence, but even of my death. During her life she was the faithful helper of my ministry. From her I never experienced the slightest hindrance."[12] Calvin, like Luther and Zwingli, had married well.

Calvin's Second Geneva Ministry

Meanwhile, back in Geneva the Guillermins (those favoring Farel glowing eyes, arrived in Geneva.[14] The city council had voted him a and Calvin) were in power again. In September 1540 the council voted to recall Calvin. He was unwilling to return. His Strassburg congregation resisted his departure; Bucer consented to it; Farel insisted on it. Although Calvin admitted he would rather endure a hundred other deaths than that cross, his discipleship is evident in his October 24 letter to Farel: "When I consider that I am not in my own power, I offer my heart a slain victim for a sacrifice to the Lord…I yield my soul chained and bound unto obedience to God."[13]

Thus on September 13, 1541, the medium-sized and lean Calvin, distinguished partially by his dark hair and beard, thin nose, and substantial salary and provided moving expenses for his family.

Calvin's opening sermon at Saint Pierre, the former cathedral, was a much-anticipated event. It disappointed those who expected a highly partisan address. Exercising great self-restraint for one so nervous and impatient, Calvin resumed preaching from the biblical chapter and verse he had used his last Sunday in 1538 and acted as if his banishment had never occurred.

By November 20 the city council and the general assembly of the Geneva church had adopted Calvin's *Ecclesiastical Ordinances,* which provide the basic structural organization of Presbyterian, Reformed, and United Church of Christ congregations yet today. Simply put, Calvin provided for four ministerial orders: "preaching pastors, teaching doctors, disciplining elders, and charity-directing deacons."[15] Calvin charged the pastors with the ministry of the word and sacraments at the frequent services of worship in Geneva's three parish churches. They met weekly to discuss theology and quarterly for administrative purposes. In 1542 there were nine pastors in Geneva.

Teachers or doctors were ordained, but their chief role was to lecture in theology and to teach in the grammar schools, which Geneva's boys and girls were compelled to attend. The teachers served the church at large. Their influence came to full fruition when in 1559 Calvin and others founded the famous Geneva Academy, forerunner of the University of Geneva. Eventually local Calvinist congregations around the world combined the office of teacher with that of pastor.

The elders were the heart of Calvin's system. Twelve in number and chosen by the city council, their major task was to enforce morality in Geneva. "Fraternal admonition," based on Hebrews 3:13, was what they named their task. Like the Radical Reformation, Calvin wanted a disciplined church; unlike them, he would have church and state cooperate in maintaining this discipline. These lay elders and ordained pastors comprised the *consistorie,* the church court before which offenders in morals or in doctrinal error came for a tongue-lashing that would hopefully result in repentance or, failing that, in punishment of various kinds. Elders outnumbered pastors on the consistorie and were considered state as well as church officials. After 1555 the consistorie became independent of the city council.

The deacons either collected alms for the poor or administered these funds on their behalf. Geneva's general hospital had been founded the year before Calvin first arrived there. Ministering to more than the sick, it also offered free lodging for strangers, served as a home for orphans and the aged, and distributed bread weekly to poor households.[16] Geneva's deacons, also elected by the city council, performed an excellent social ministry.

Calvin's reform of Geneva was rigorous. He and his followers forebade gambling and dancing, suppressed prostitution, and curbed excessive drinking by closing taverns at a decent hour. The consistorie heard cases every Thursday morning dealing with violations of such rules, as well as accusations of failure to attend church, profanity, drunkenness, adultery, wife-beating, and so on. Punishments leveled against the unrepentant included banishment or, in extreme cases, the death penalty.

Quite naturally, many Genevese highly resented these checks on their freedom. Antagonism against Calvin ran high. Some people out of disrespect for the reformer named their dogs after him. Some shortened his name to Cain. Still others refused to receive the Lord's Supper, stating that their hatred of Calvin was the reason.[17] Calvin named the opposition party the "Libertines" because they scorned law. Despite their antagonism, Calvin uncompromisingly held to his penchant for moral order and decency. He did not lack courage. Once when a Libertine-aroused armed mob gathered to intimidate the city council, Calvin bared his breast crying out, "If you must shed blood, let mine be the first." This bold action won a hearing and prevented a riot, but not long after the timid scholar wrote, "I wish God would grant me my discharge."[18]

Calvin ministered under the threat of a second banishment from Geneva. The Libertines constantly sought a city council majority with which to end his dominance over the city. Several celebrated test cases emerged, one regarding Sebastian Castellio, a humanist scholar turned Protestant. Arriving in Geneva in 1542, he became rector of Calvin's school. Unable to support his large family on a teacher's salary, Castellio sought ordination in order to supplement his income. Calvin offered a salary increase but not ordination, due to Castellio's unorthodox scriptural interpretations. The council banished Castellio in 1544. Another banishment case, Jerome Bolsec, a physician who denounced Calvin's doctrine of predestination as being absurd and false, retaliated by publishing a vilifying and unfair biography of Calvin.

The most celebrated antagonist to face Calvin was Michael Servetus, a Spaniard educated in theology, law, and medicine. Servetus and Calvin had met as university students. The former had great speculative gifts and was widely traveled. As a thinker he was learned, original, and resourceful, if disorderly. In 1531 he published *On the Errors of the Doctrine of the Trinity* and in 1533 his *Restitution of Christianity*, in which he denied infant baptism, original sin, the Trinity, and the divine nature of Christ.

The Roman Catholics tried and sentenced Servetus to death in Lyon according to a sixth-century law that made denial of the doctrines of the Trinity and infant baptism punishable by death. Servetus escaped, and in August 1553 he appeared in Geneva. He was recognized and arrested. Now the Libertines saw their chance to unseat Calvin by defending Servetus. Calvin unsuccessfully tried to get Servetus to recant. At his trial, the latter, exasperated and impudent, demanded that Calvin be tried instead. Calvin had consulted with other Swiss Protestant cities regarding Servetus's penalty. From Zurich and Bern came the recommendation of the death penalty. When the city council found Servetus guilty of spreading heresy and condemned him to die by burning, Calvin fruitlessly sought to get the sentence commuted to beheading. On October 27, 1553, Servetus died at the stake. From the flames came his prayer, "O Jesus, thou Son of the eternal God, have pity on me." He might have gone unpunished had he prayed, "Jesus, eternal Son of God." He misplaced the adjective *eternal*.[19]

With the death of Servetus and the favorable election of 1555, the political opposition to Calvin in Geneva expired. The large numbers of Huguenots who fled France for the security of Geneva now constituted increasingly strong support. Calvin's publications continued, including a commentary on every New Testament book except Revelation and on many Old Testament books. They would eventually fill forty-nine volumes. The Geneva Academy, at Calvin's death, had twelve hundred students in its undergraduate gymnasium, and three hundred pursuing theological studies. Many of the latter became the Calvinist missionaries sent into other European countries. Before he died, Calvin knew of the growing success of John Knox in making Scotland Presbyterian, of the German Calvinist *Heidelberg Catechism* of 1563, of the coming bloody struggle for independence from Spain of the Dutch Calvinists under William of Orange (1533–84), of the penetration of his teaching into Hungary and, for a time, Poland, and of the 150 missions that in 1561 alone were sent into his native France.

Calvin, who had suffered from many illnesses across the years, succumbed to tuberculosis in 1564. At his request, he was buried in an unmarked grave in Geneva. There was to be no Calvin memorial. All glory goes to God alone. The reformer was a complicated man, carrying within him a terrible temper, a hatred of disorder, and the ability to make harsh judgments, alongside brilliance of mind, strong resolve, and a genuine capacity for friendship. He appreciated art, music, and good food and drink, but all in moderation. A contemporary called him "a bow always strung."[20] Calvin never wanted the Lord to find him idle. From his deep faith in God, his strong determination that Geneva be reformed, and his prolific writings emerged a definitive system of Protestant theology and church government.

CALVIN'S UNDERSTANDING OF THE CHRISTIAN FAITH

The theological term most identified with John Calvin is *predestination,* a doctrine that the Genevan reformer tenaciously taught and defended. Predestination is not, however, the foundation of Calvin's theology. Calvin's theology rests on the sovereignty of God.

Calvin opened his *Institutes* by saying that nearly all the wisdom we possess consists of two parts: knowledge of God and of ourselves. These are interwoven. If we do not know ourselves we have no knowledge of God; conversely, without knowledge of God we cannot know ourselves. Despite the connection between these two themes, right teaching requires that we discuss God first and then proceed to analyze ourselves.[21]

The only way people can know God, said Calvin, is for divine revelation to teach them. To be sure, people can learn about God by observing how God works in "this glorious theater" of the universe. Calvin thus made a place for natural theology but warned immediately that the human mind is prone to forgetfulness, has a tendency to every kind of error, and lusts after the opportunity to create new and artificial religions.[22] When people indulge in their curiosity about God, they enter a *labyrinth* (a favorite word of Calvin). Thus, they should not seek God anywhere other than in the divine word.[23]

The Word of God, for Calvin, was Jesus Christ, who is God's everlasting wisdom, author of all prophecies and oracles, eternal from the beginning and by whom all things were made.[24] The word of God is also the divine message in scripture. In the *Geneva Catechism,* a portion of the dialogue between minister and child reads:

M: By what road does one come to such blessedness?

C: To this end God has left us his sacred Word. For spiritual doctrine is a kind of door, by which we enter into his celestial Kingdom.

M: Where must we seek this Word?

C: In the Holy Scriptures in which it is contained.[25]

Calvin's understanding that the word of God is contained in scripture allowed him to posit several key truths about God's self-revelation. One is that Christ, the Word of words, encounters us in scripture. Another is that this revelation is not automatically available in Bible reading; only those who have the Holy Spirit, the inner teacher, can receive it. "For as God alone is a fit witness of himself in his Word, so also the Word will not find acceptance in men's hearts before it is sealed by the inward testimony of the Spirit."[26] A balance thus exists between holy scripture and the Holy Spirit. The Holy Spirit who inspired the scriptures must also inspire our hearts to receive the divine word in the scriptures; on the other hand, Christians must measure all inspirations they receive by holy scripture since the Holy Spirit would never give conflicting testimony.

Calvin used the scriptures primarily as the source of saving doctrine. This approach enabled him to avoid some of the intricacies of textual interpretation and to focus on the basic truths of God's word. The reformer was unsure whether the patriarchs knew God through visions and oracles or through human instrumentality. Nonetheless, God revealed what they should hand down to their posterity. Undoubtedly God had imparted true doctrine to them. They themselves were convinced that what they had learned had come from God.[27]

Calvin was certain that humanity could fulfill its need to know God only by accepting divine revelation in the holy scriptures. He wrote that it was fine for people to use their eyes to contemplate God in nature, but they profited all the more from using their ears to hear the divine word.[28]

What does scripture reveal of God? God is sovereign, absolute Lord, the all-determining one. God is transcendent and eternal. God created and superintends the universe. The will of God is good. Calvin made much of God's providence. Faith tells us that if God created the universe, God must also sustain, nourish, and care for it. God rules the universe in general but also each person individually. The afflictions that people assign to fate or chance are really things that happen through God's command or permission. God foresees how long each person will live. Providence is God's wonderful way of governing the world. Even if we call God's governance an "abyss" (another favorite Calvin word) because its way is hidden from us, we still ought to adore it reverently.[29] Calvin saw this as genuine confidence for the future. God's will is not capricious, cruel, blind fate. We can trust it. After all, the great sweetness of God's beneficence and goodness invites us to love and serve God with all our hearts.[30]

Against the inscrutable wisdom and justice of God, humanity stands in shabby comparison. The original righteousness with which God created humanity, Adam's fall destroyed. This alienated the human race from God. If God's image was not totally annihilated in Adam's fall, it was terribly deformed.[31] Thus our sin does not emerge from our nature but from the corruption of our nature.[32]

Because of original sin inherited from Adam and Eve, each person suffers from a hereditary depravity and corruption of nature that makes him or her liable to God's wrath.[33] This all stems from our first parents' disobedience, the beginning of all evils.[34] As a result, our intellect is blind; our will is full of corrupt affections; and our bodily strength tends toward iniquity.[35] For this reason, human beings do not have the free will to turn to God.

To be sure, humanity in its original state of innocence did enjoy free will to choose what is good and to attain eternal life. The creator, however, did not fashion people who could not or would not sin. Though they possessed the ability to avoid sin, they did not possess the will to exercise it. As a result, Adam and Eve fell easily into sin.[36] Their descendants now sin of necessity, not because they are deprived of will, but of a *sound* will.[37] Calvin admitted that it was absurd and a contradiction, but the Fall is something for which people through Adam are responsible and which, on the other hand, proceeded from the "admirable wisdom of God" for the humiliation of the human race.[38] If God superintends the universe and all that happens in it, it logically follows that the fall of Adam and Eve did not occur without God's knowledge and involvement.

Just as Calvin did not hesitate to present God as responsible for the human sin problem, so he did not shrink from seeing sin in infants and little children, whom many deem innocent until some age of accountability. Infants, carrying the condemnation of original sin from their mothers' wombs, are guilty not only of another's sin but of their own. Even though they have not yet produced the results of their iniquities, they will do so because their whole nature has been corrupted.[39]

Against this dour and pessimistic view of the human condition, Calvin affirmed the good news of God in Christ to which he gave this summary: "The doctrine of the gospel, in few words, is this: to know God, and put our whole trust in Him: and to know by what means He is our Savior: namely, in the person of our Lord Jesus Christ, His only begotten Son, who died for our justification."[40]

A word Calvin used frequently to describe the God/human relationship in the world is *accommodation*. God needs to be self-accommodating in relationship to the world, which cannot stand direct contact with the radiance of the divine glory. Thus in the divine revelation in scripture God "accommodates himself to our ignorance," using figures and metaphors to address us "according to the measure of our capacities."[41] Scholars have humorously referred to Calvin's understanding of God's use of "baby-talk" to address us through the scriptures. This concept allowed Calvin to overlook scientific errors in scripture. If God needed to talk down to our level of comprehension, it did not matter if the scriptures contained scientific errors.[42]

The incarnation of our Lord was the same. God's salvation is available to the world only in Jesus Christ, the only begotten and eternal Son of God. Calvin quoted the church father Irenaeus: "The Father, himself infinite, becomes finite in the Son, for he has accommodated himself to our little measure lest our minds be overwhelmed by the immensity of his glory."[43] Calvin's understanding of Christ was orthodox. Our Lord is both God and human, two natures in one person. He made satisfaction on the cross for human sin, was resurrected from the dead, and ascended to the right hand of God. It was when Calvin raised the question, "For whom did Christ die?" that he entered into serious theological controversy.

The doctrine of predestination did not originate with Calvin. *Predestination* and *election* are biblical terms. Certain church fathers, preeminently Augustine (354–430), taught it. The great medieval Roman Catholic theologian, Thomas Aquinas (c. 1225–74), paid considerable attention to it, albeit in a somewhat modified way. Calvin came to it largely through his reading of Augustine and Luther. About 350 quotations from Augustine appear in Calvin's *Institutes*. Augustine taught that human nature is so corrupt and caught up in "self-love" that it cannot turn to God. Therefore, people whom God elects apart from human merit God enables to persevere in the way of salvation. God relinquishes the nonelect to their forlorn fate.

Calvin admitted that the doctrine of predestination was a baffling question. Those who probe into it are searching into the secrets of God's will that we are to revere but not understand. Whatever we say in this regard should be limited only to what scripture teaches. With a logician's sharp capacity for clarity and distinction, the reformer offered this definition: "We call predestination God's eternal decree by which he determined with himself what he willed to become of each man. For all are not created in equal condition; rather, eternal life is foreordained for some, eternal damnation for others. Therefore, as any man has been created to one or the other of these ends, we speak of him as predestined to life or to death."[44]

Recognizing how controversial this subject was, Calvin did not include it in his catechism for children. He was careful when using it in sermons. However, he believed that it was the biblical doctrine that in clearest fashion depicted the impotence of humankind regarding salvation and the manner in which God's grace alone saves us.

Some of Calvin's disciples may have departed from his strong Christological basis for the doctrine of predestination and may, thus, have drawn sharper and more severe conclusions on this issue than he intended. It must be conceded, however, that the doctrine that God alone chooses people for salvation or damnation is deeply rooted in the reformer's thought.

Several observations about Calvin's predestinarian teaching may be helpful. First of all, predestination is the most radical doctrine of salvation by grace alone found in Christian theology. It is a direct threat to any form of works righteousness. It reminds those who intend to achieve merit before God through any thought, word, or deed they perform to "forget it"! Salvation comes about by God's choice and power as a gracious (undeserved and unmerited) gift, and we can only understand and receive it as such.

Second, predestination for Calvin had practical ramifications. It explained how people came to salvation. Calvin believed that people's experience bore out his teaching.

Third, Calvin saw predestination to be centered in the work of Christ. Interestingly, in his first edition of the *Institutes* he located predestination under the doctrine of God's providence; but in the 1559 edition, he treated providence at the end of the section dealing with the doctrine of God and predestination came in the sections on salvation.[45] The latter clearly related to salvation. Predestination, he believed, was tightly interwoven with Christ. Virtually all the New Testament passages Calvin used to support the doctrine of predestination spoke of the person and work of Christ; for example, John 6:44, 10:28–29, 15:16; Romans 9–11; Ephesians 1:4–5; Colossians 1:12; and 1 Peter 1:2. Even in John 3:16, where our Lord announced that everyone who believes in Christ "may not perish but may have eternal life," Calvin demurred in his interpretation: "Moreover, let us remember that although life is promised generally to all who believe in Christ, faith is not common to all. Christ is open to all and displayed to all, but God opens the eyes only of the elect that they may seek Him by faith."[46]

While this interpretation may not satisfy most Christians today, we cannot escape the fact that Calvin believed God elected people to salvation in and through Jesus Christ. For believers, Christ was the assurance of their salvation. Through Christ also came their election, "which was determined by grace before the foundation of the world."[47]

A fourth noteworthy connection exists between predestination or election and faith. Christian faith, for Calvin, and for Luther and Zwingli, was trust. One of Calvin's many fine definitions of faith bears repetition: "Now we shall possess a right definition of faith if we call it a firm and certain knowledge of God's benevolence toward us, founded upon the truth of the freely given promise in Christ, both revealed to our minds and sealed upon our hearts through the Holy Spirit."[48]

Aside from the strong trinitarian component here, we find the powerful role of the Holy Spirit in bringing persons to faith. Calvin refined this by stating that, according to Paul in Ephesians 1:3-4, the mother of faith is election.[49] This being the case, God does not elect people for salvation because they believe; rather, they believe because God elects them. Faith is a gift of God through the Holy Spirit. Calvin affirmed that we have a certainty of our election when we receive God's doctrine with obedience and faith, rest ourselves upon the divine promises, and accept the offer to be taken as God's children.[50]

One might expect that persons who believed they were among the elect could easily move into pride and careless living. Not according to Calvin. Lest believers think they "had it made" because God had chosen them for salvation, Calvin was quick to remind them that "holiness, innocence, and every virtue…are the fruit of election."[51]

In order to insure that Christians would bring forth the fruits of righteousness in their daily living, Calvin instituted what has come to be known as his "third use of the law." He agreed with Luther regarding the law's first two "uses": that the law of God judges people in their unrighteousness, helping drive the elect to God's mercy in Christ, and that the law in its restraint of evil and unjust people makes human society possible. The "third use of the law" is its instilling daily instruction in believers so that they can progress toward a purer knowledge of God's will.[52] It is for their sanctification. The law in its third use reveals how the elect are to live disciplined lives in Christ. Calvin did not expect his followers to reach perfection in this life, but he did intend for them to walk on a very short leash in the way God had revealed to them in the law.[53] Grace alone saves the elect, but the law guides their life in Christ.

Calvin's definition of the church is often quoted: "Wherever we see the Word of God purely preached and heard, and the sacraments administered according to Christ's institution, there, it is not to be doubted, a church of God exists" (Eph. 2:20).[54] Like the third-century church father Cyprian, Calvin looked upon the church as the mother of believers. He wrote appreciatively,

> For there is no other way to enter into life unless this mother conceive us in her womb, give us birth, nourish us at her breast, and lastly, unless she keep us under her care and guidance until, putting off mortal flesh, we become like the angels [Matt. 22:30]. Our weakness does not allow us to be dismissed from her school until we have been pupils all our lives. Furthermore, away from her bosom one cannot hope for any forgiveness of sins or any salvation.[55]

With the doctrine of predestination looming in the background, Calvin distinguished between the church as visible and invisible. The church as mother is the visible church on earth, locally and universally. It is the totality of those who confess Christ. Not all these people are elect; Calvin referred to the remainder as hypocrites. He did not presume to know who the elect were. God alone knows this and, in Christ, calls people to salvation. Here again, however, God accommodates our capacity by giving us a "charitable judgment" whereby we can recognize as church members those who confess their faith, live exemplary lives, partake of the sacraments, and profess the same God and Christ as we do.[56]

In reality, however, the visible church, the gathered body of believers, is the church as we see it; the invisible church, the true church of the elect, is the church as God sees it. The preaching of the word and the sacraments call forth the former. It contains nonelect hypocrites and waits for elect sinners outside its walls to enter in, as they eventually must. In the meantime, it must look seriously to its doctrine and the discipline of its people. Calvin maintained a high doctrine of the church throughout his career.

Just as he placed great importance on the preaching and teaching of the word of God, so Calvin highly valued the sacraments, which were also testimonies of God's grace to us through the use of outward signs such as water, bread, and wine. He declared that if faith rests on the word of God as its foundation, the pillars on which it rests all the more firmly are the sacraments.[57]

The reformer used a rich array of metaphors to describe the sacraments. Accommodating our earthbound limitations, God uses the sacraments as signs (visible things conveying spiritual truth) to prop up our weak faith. The sacraments are seals that confirm the word the way a seal on an official document authenticates the message it contains. Following Augustine, Calvin regarded a sacrament as a visible word, a painted picture of God's promised grace.[58] The Holy Spirit makes sacramental grace effective for the elect.

For Calvin, baptism is the sign of initiation into the covenant people of God, just as circumcision was in the Hebrew community. It signifies washing and cleansing in Christ's blood. It shows forth our dying with Christ and rising to new life in him. Infants born into

Christian homes are to be baptized and thus given the mark of the covenant and their cleansing in Christ.

Calvin stood between Luther and Zwingli regarding the Lord's Supper. He agreed with Zwingli that Christ's body had ascended into heaven and could not be present in the bread and wine. With Luther, however, he was not content that the Supper be a bare memorial and a testimony of faith that Christians share with one another while communing at the Lord's table. Instead, Calvin affirmed that Christ was spiritually present in the bread and wine. Our Lord, to be sure, has physically ascended into heaven, but since the kingdom knows no limits by time and space, the Holy Spirit lifts our eyes and minds to the ascended Christ as we eat and drink in faith at Christ's table.[59] The Lord's Supper serves to "nourish, refresh, strengthen, and gladden" Christians.[60]

CALVIN'S INSIGHTS FOR CHRISTIAN LIVING

Most Christians today have departed from the seemingly austere and unfair picture of God provided by Calvin's doctrine of predestination. Nevertheless, basic truths in the Genevan reformer's teachings can inform and nurture our faith here at the beginning of the third Christian millennium.

One of these is Calvin's bold confidence that Christians are to live for God's glory and not their own. Many older Protestants will recognize the opening question and answer in the *Presbyterian Catechism:* "Question: What is the chief end of man? Answer: Man's chief end is to glorify God, and to enjoy him forever."[61]

Over three centuries several million young people, both within and beyond the Reformed tradition, memorized this brief passage as part of their religious training. As a result they encountered one of Calvin's fundamental precepts. We are not placed on this earth for our own human self-actualization and self-gratification. Instead, we are here to live for the glory of God, who created us. This theme repeatedly appears in holy scripture. For example, in Psalm 3:3, David calls God "a shield around me, my glory, and the one who lifts up my head." Our Lord challenged the disciples to let their light shine before others "so that they may see your good works and give glory to your Father in heaven" (Matt. 5:16). The Apostle Paul named Abraham a model disciple, noting that "no distrust made him waver concerning the promise of God, but he grew strong in his faith as he gave glory to God" (Rom. 4:20).

Calvin emphasized the biblical theme of our exalting God's glory because of who God is. In his definitive letter to Cardinal Sadoleto in 1539, he observed, "It is not very sound theology to confine a man's thoughts so much to himself, and not to set before him, as the prime motive of his existence, zeal to illustrate the glory of God. For we are born first of all for God, and not for ourselves."[62]

We see here another reason for people to glorify God. It is good for our souls. It lifts our hearts and minds off ourselves and on to God, who is really the center of our being. Calvin believed that our being is nothing but existence in God.[63] When we repent we depart from ourselves and turn to God.[64]

The emphasis on living for God's glory injected something of a healthy objectivity into Calvin's understanding of the Christian life. Believers were not constantly to assess their feelings and performance. The reformer went so far as to say that for persons to contemplate themselves was sure damnation. Those, however, who recognize that Christ with all his benefits has been imparted to them, rejoice that his salvation has wiped out their condemnation.[65]

Calvin admitted that it is not easy for believers to disregard themselves and focus on God. They might even undergo occasional interruptions of faith. Despite these interruptions he understood one thing very well. Those who fix their eyes, hearts, and minds on the divine in preference to the human; who are more concerned that God get the glory for their salvation, success, and well-being than they themselves; and who are not boastful because they understand life and salvation as gifts from God and not human achievements—such persons will have things in proper perspective and live to the glory of God, as the creator intended. It is only in fellowship with God that human beings achieve their highest good.[66]

Another of Calvin's contributions to the understanding of Christian living parallels his high doctrine of God. It is his low estimate of human ability to get right with God. The Genevan reformer did not detest humankind, as he has often been accused. He recognized that "reason is proper to our nature" and that God's common grace endows people with the many gifts that enable them to succeed in the arts and sciences, in government and business, and in other reputable activities of life.[67] Nonetheless, Calvin was realistic about human nature, emphasizing that sin is the fatal disease from which it suffers.[68] Therefore, he attacked his opponents for intoxicating people with perverse opinions of their own virtues. This led them to give God no more glory for their salvation than they did themselves. It led people, in large measure, to depend on themselves. The reformer claimed that he and his followers, theologically at least, laid people "completely prostrate" so that, aware of their insufficiency in spiritual matters, they would trust God alone for salvation.[69] A profound reliance on God and an exhilarating freedom from self are the rewards for those who are saved, as Calvin put it, "out of mere grace."[70]

Many persons today, however, wanting to own their involvement and participation in the relationship with God, find it demeaning to say that in salvation "God in Christ does it all." Their sentiments are genuine. Calvin would encourage such persons, however, to see salvation from sin, guilt, and eternal death as similar to rescue from drowning. If a nonswimmer ventures into a body of water and is suddenly and helplessly engulfed in depths that bring on stark terror, that person wants and needs a life preserver to land within clutching distance. Thus, by doing no more than ingloriously grabbing hold and hanging on, he or she enjoys rescue from harm's way exclusively by outside help. Calvin, like Luther and Zwingli, saw the human race as "nonswimmers" as far as salvation is concerned. Human potential is ineffective for salvation.

Calvin's understanding of salvation resulted in another of his major doctrines regarding Christian living. Christ's followers are to exhibit grateful obedience. Coupling his emphases on humanity's need to glorify God with his stress on the third use of the law could only lead Calvin to extol the joys and benefits of obedience. Evidence of our progressing in the Christian life is apparent when, forgetting ourselves and subordinating our self-concern, we seek to devote ourselves fully to God and God's commandments.[71] The reformer believed that nothing pleases God more than obedience.[72]

Calvin's own life supported these contentions. He resisted ministerial calls to Geneva, Strassburg, and Geneva; yielding only when others convinced him that these invitations were God's will. He referred to his Strassburg ministry, saying, "Yet I was led as it were by force."[73]

Balancing Calvin's concern that Christians live obedient lives was his stress on gratitude as the motivation by which they should do this. People will choose to live obedient lives much more from gratitude than from command or even exhortation. Calvin understood that the finest worship of God is the celebration of God's goodness by giving thanks.[74] People are moved to thanksgiving when they hear a recital of what God has done for them. Gratitude is a basic foundation for discipleship.

Furthermore, obedience comes easier if people remember who they are. Following the Apostle Paul's admonition to his Christian readers (Rom. 12:1–2) that they should present their bodies as living sacrifices to God and thus seek to do the divine will, the reformer concluded that we are not our own masters but belong to God. The career choices that he himself made are summarized by lines that lyrically describe the reformer's own God-relationship:

> If we, then, are not our own (1 Cor. 6:19) but the Lord's, it is clear what error we must flee, and whither we must direct all the acts of our life.
>
> We are not our own: let not our reason nor our will, therefore, sway our plans and deeds. We are not our own: let us therefore not set it as our goal to seek what is expedient for us according to the flesh. We are not our own: insofar as we can, let us therefore forget ourselves and all that is ours.
>
> Conversely, we are God's: let us therefore live for him and die for him. We are God's: let his wisdom and will therefore rule all our actions. We are God's: let all the parts of our life accordingly strive toward him as our only lawful goal (Romans 14:8; cf. 1 Cor. 6:19). O how much has that man profited who, having been taught that he is not his own, has taken away dominion and rule from his own reason that he may yield it to God! For, as consulting our self-interest is the pestilence that most effectively leads to our destruction, so the sole haven of salvation is to be wise in nothing and to will nothing through ourselves but to following the leading of the Lord alone.[75]

Obedience, fueled by gratitude, is also made possible by humility and self-denial.

A last contribution Calvin made to this understanding of the Christian life is the focus on active involvement in the world. This too he sourced in the Christian's need to live for the glory of God as well as the necessity for alleviating human suffering. People so disinterested in their own welfare and intent on obeying God's will are neither timid nor lazy. Calvin's own active and turbulent ministry was a case in point. He ruled Geneva from his pulpit, but he also frequently attended the council meetings at city hall to get his social and political ideas adopted. He never hesitated to apply the gospel to the affairs of everyday life. Indeed, in the last pages of his *Institutes* he dealt with political issues. Heeding the mandate of Romans 13:1-2, he urged people to be obedient under and even to suffer the rule of tyrannical monarchs. However, he left the door to revolution ever so slightly ajar with his summons to "the magistrates of the people" to protect the latter from the fierce licentiousness of their rulers. Beyond that, Christians are to resist rulers when, in order to obey them, they would have to disobey God.[76]

Since Calvin's time his followers have conspicuously opposed political and social injustices. Admittedly, they have done this neither consistently nor gently. Nonetheless, recall the Puritan Revolution in seventeenth-century England, our own strongly Calvinist-led American Revolution a century later (when King George III reportedly greeted the news of the battles of Lexington and Concord with the retort that they were "Presbyterian riots"), and the uprisings in Hungary in the last two centuries. Lajos Kossuth, who led the unsuccessful Hungarian revolution against the Hapsburg monarchy in 1848, and Jan Palemeter, an instigator of the 1956 uprising against Communism, were products of the Calvinist tradition. More recently, the

Reverend Laszlo Tokes and his ethnic Hungarian Reformed congregation in Romania in 1989–90 offered determined resistance that led to the toppling of the cruel Ceausescu dictatorship. Perhaps Lord Macaulay put it most aptly when he observed that the English Puritans knelt humbly before their God and set their feet upon the necks of kings.[77] A seventeenth-century observer remarked, "I had rather meet coming against me a whole regiment with drawn swords than one Calvinist convinced that he is doing the will of God."[78] This exaggeration pays tribute to the iron resolve so often associated with Calvinism. It depicts a courageous involvement clearly drawn from the life and teaching of the reformer of Geneva.

In Geneva to this day stands the International Monument of Reformation, a wall one hundred meters long, built in 1909, the four-hundredth anniversary of Calvin's birth. Six smaller statues along the wall represent lesser-known Calvinist leaders of the sixteenth and seventeenth centuries. In the center, however, are four six-meter-high statues of the four Calvinist reformers who were present in Geneva in 1559: William Farel, John Calvin, Theodore Beza (Calvin's successor), and John Knox, the reformer of Scotland. All four hold a book in their hands—three of them the holy scriptures. Beza holds the rules of the Geneva Academy, founded that year. The statue of Calvin is especially notable. He stands a little ahead of the others as if he were carrying them and the whole church forward into the Reformation. Beyond that, with two fingers, he holds the Bible open, as if he were ready to cite chapter and verse. The huge letters *Post Tenebras Lux* ("After the darkness, light") that surround the main figures are the motto of Geneva. They also underscore the symbolism of Calvin's open Bible—that the light the reformers had to share was not theirs, but that redemptive word from God they found only in the pages of holy scripture.[79]

A PRAYER OF JOHN CALVIN

Almighty God, as nothing is better for us or more necessary for our chief happiness than to depend on thy Word, for that is a sure pledge of thy good will towards us, grant that, as thou hast favored us with so singular a benefit, we may be attentive to hear thee and submit ourselves to thee in true fear, meekness, and humility. May we be prepared in the spirit of meekness to receive whatever proceeds from thee, and may thy Word not only be precious to us, but also sweet and delightful, until we shall enjoy the perfection of that life which thine only-begotten Son has procured for us by his own blood. Amen.[80]

FOR PERSONAL OR GROUP REFLECTION

1. Think about Calvin's understanding of obedience in the life of those who want to follow Christ. How have you heard God's call in your life and how have you obeyed?

2. Calvin was involved in a rigorous reform of Geneva. In what ways do you see Christians and the church influencing and shaping values and society today?

3. Reflect on Calvin's writings that God is self-accommodating in relationship to the world because we could not understand or respond to the true radiance of divine glory. What parts of scripture and faith are most difficult for you? Where do you struggle for understanding?

4. What about John Calvin might have attracted you to him? repelled you?

5. How might Calvin's life story and his teachings have affected your understanding of Christian discipleship?

6. How might we use the teeter-totter idea to describe Calvin's sense of balance between the authority of holy scripture and that of the Holy Spirit? How have you experienced the power of the Holy Spirit in the reading and understanding of scripture?

7. How does your view of God compare to Calvin's portrayal of a sovereign God?

8. What does *sin* mean to you, and how does your understanding of it compare with Calvin's writings on original sin?

9. Do you agree that Calvin's views on predestination paint a radical picture of grace? If we say that faith is a gift of God and further say that only those who believe will be saved (John 3:16), are we getting a bit close to predestination?

10. Calvin emphasized that as Christians "we are not our own"? Would we be better Christians if we lived more in God through Christ than in ourselves? How can we do that? What might be the results if we took this understanding seriously?

MENNO
SIMONS

CHAPTER 4

"The Pressing Cross of Christ"

THE LIFE AND MINISTRY
OF MENNO SIMONS

*E*lizabeth Dirks was an Anabaptist teacher who was arrested in her native Holland. When she refused to tell who her parents were, who had baptized her, or whom she had taught in her new way of life, the authorities applied screws to her hands and legs. When torture failed to break her resolve, she was drowned in a sack on March 27, 1549.[1]

Dirk Willems, a Dutchman and suspected Anabaptist, fled for his life across a frozen lake. When his pursuer broke through the ice, Willems, forsaking his own freedom, turned and pulled his enemy to safety. Before he could escape, Willems was captured by onlookers. At his trial he admitted to having been rebaptized and to holding secret meetings in his home, at which several other persons had been rebaptized. His stubborn persistence in his faith led to his martyrdom by fire on May 16, 1569.[2]

Hans Bret was a confectioner in an Antwerp bakery. A serious Bible student, he spent his Sunday afternoons instructing recent converts to prepare them for baptism. Arrested and imprisoned in the Antwerp castle dungeon, Bret sent letters to his relatives describing his interrogation. When he was judged and sentenced to death, an iron clamp was screwed over his tongue, the end of which was burned with a hot iron. The resultant swelling was to prevent Bret from speaking to the crowd that gathered to watch him die. He was burned at the stake on January 4, 1577.[3]

Who were these people, and why were they willing to suffer torture and death? The answer to this question lies simply in the understanding they had of the Reformation.

Historians often refer to the work of Luther, Calvin, and Zwingli as the "magisterial Reformation" because they established their movements with the support of the state or governing authorities. This was also true of the Anglican Reformation. The magisterial Reformation sought to reform the Roman Catholic church as a whole, with theological, ethical, and liturgical change envisioned for all people in a given area. Such far-reaching intentions quite naturally involved existing political structures. All these assumed the continuance of a state-supported Christianity that had dominated Europe since the emperor Constantine in the fourth century became a Christian and, with his descendants, began establishing Christianity as the only viable religious expression for Europe's people.

THE RADICAL REFORMATION

During the Reformation, however, a group of people emerged who greeted this state-supported, established Christianity with active disapproval. Reading the same Bible and acknowledging the same tradition as did those involved in the magisterial Reformation, these dissidents pleaded instead for a change in understanding of the Christian life and consequently of the nature and work of the church. What they really sought was a return to early Christianity, when the church existed as a free, albeit persecuted, body within the Roman

Empire; when Christians, having experienced the new birth the Savior had promised, were empowered to follow him in a discipleship that was intentional and perhaps costly; when the early church, instead of admitting seekers on a vast, open scale that required of them little evidence of faith and love, maintained high admission standards followed by rigorous disciplines in keeping with the imitation of Christ. Emerging in the 1520s, these persons who held to the model of the early church were called "the left wing of the Reformation" or "the Radical Reformation." George Huntston Williams coined the latter term and notes four major themes that characterized this movement.[4]

Restitution of the New Testament Church

These persons envisioned not the Reformation but the restitution of the church. The Golden Age to which these radicals looked backward was the church as it was formed in the first three centuries after Christ. Now, as emissaries of the true church, which had been in dispersion for twelve centuries, they were committed to ushering in the New Age, by which the fall of the church would be reversed.[5] Their laments concerning the church's worldliness, formalism, clericalism, governmental dependence, support of war, and lust for power and wealth suggested what the radical reformers viewed as marks of the church's fall. Thus, the radicals grew impatient with what they felt were the cautious, halfway reforms of Luther and Zwingli. One observer said that Luther "broke the pope's pitcher, but kept the pieces in his hands."[6] Reformation of a church so corrupted was impossible; the church of the New Testament needed restoration to the purity it possessed in the days before Constantine's time.

Separation of Church and State

The Radical Reformation was the great proponent of separation of church and state, later a distinguishing mark of democracy in the United States of America. These people believed in religious liberty, partially because they espoused the doctrine of the freedom of the will. Balthasar Hubmaier's 1527 treatise, *The Freedom of the Will*, admitted that through the fall of Adam and Eve human beings were sorely wounded in the flesh. Still, the grace of God was like a wedding or a dinner invitation empowering people to choose. God compels no one except "by the sending and summoning of his Word."[7] God's persuasive appeal to the human race endowed with free will totally eliminated the place for any form of religious oppression. State-compelled church adherence was bad theology as well as bad politics.

The radicals' understanding of the church was a natural outgrowth of this free will. If individuals were free to accept or reject God's grace, so the faith community must also be free of any societal control. Franklin Littell contended that the two notes characterizing the radical reformers' view of the church were that the church had to be a voluntary association of persons who intentionally became a part of its fellowship and that it must pattern itself after the New Testament in its faith and communal organization.[8]

The church should not only be free of state support or control, it should also be pure. Against the large, lax, and undisciplined Roman Catholic, Lutheran, and Zwinglian churches, the left-wing reformers projected a small, regenerated church, separate from society and disciplined in its daily life. Menno Simons, a leader in this movement, more than once admitted to a certain weakness and error in the daily walk of himself and his followers.[9] This did not prevent him, however, from setting high standards for his followers:

"Therefore, no one can be a profitable member in this most holy, glorious, and pure body of Christ who is not believing, regenerate, converted, changed and renewed; who is not kind, generous, merciful, pitying, chaste, sober, humble, patient, long-suffering, just, constant, heavenly and spiritually minded with Christ."[10]

Menno Simons and his Radical Reformation colleagues desired a church constituted by people seriously given to living the new life in Christ. Therefore, they adopted strict standards by which persons were admitted into the church (believers' baptism) and by which they were permitted to stay in (the ban).

The radical reformers saw infant baptism as the corrupter of the church. It opened the church's doors to all kinds of people lacking the necessary regeneration for new life in Christ. Menno Simons called infant baptism "a horrible stench and abomination before God."[11] Infants were not rational beings; they could not understand or accept God's word of saving grace. Moreover, there was no danger should infants die unbaptized before they had reached the age of accountability. They were covered by Christ's atonement. Believers' baptism, however, bolstered the idea of a holy, disciplined church.

Baptism, according to the Radical Reformation, did not convey grace; it was a sign that persons had by faith received God's redeeming grace and wished now to be incorporated into the people of God, among whom they were expected to grow in faith and obedience. Faith had to precede baptism, for by faith people were regenerated or born again. Menno Simons clearly stated this understanding:

> Because holy Christian baptism is a washing of regeneration, according to the doctrine of Paul, therefore none can be washed therewith to the pleasure and will of God save those who are regenerated through the Word of God. For we are

not regenerated because we are baptized, as may be perceived in the infants who have been baptized; but we are baptized because we are regenerated by faith in God's Word. For regeneration is not the result of baptism, but baptism the result of regeneration.[12]

The church could be faithful in God's sight if it opened its doors only to those who had first heard the word of God, believed it, were born anew, and made a willing decision to follow Christ in the company of the committed.

Their detractors called these people Anabaptists, which meant that they were "baptizing again." The Radical Reformation people denied that they were practicing rebaptism since, in their estimation, their baptism as infants, performed without their conscious consent, was no baptism at all. It was merely "a dipping in the Romish bath."[13]

While believers' baptism carefully screened those who sought admission to the church, the ban (exclusion from the Lord's Supper and shunning by fellow believers) served to discipline any church members who might go astray. Church leaders followed closely the threefold disciplinary steps provided by our Lord in Matthew 18.[14] The radicals deemed the ban necessary to discipline any lapsed members of the community. They intended that it bring them to repentance and prevent a congregation from being shamed by open transgressions.[15] The kinds of offenses leading to the ban were heavy drinking, adultery, swearing of oaths, marriage to an unbeliever, teaching false doctrines, unrelieved quarreling with one's spouse, and embezzlement of the congregation's money.[16]

The ban exerted heavy social pressures on wayward members in Radical Reformation congregations. It became particularly difficult when persons were called to shun family members on whom the ban of the church had been laid. Shunning interfered with delicate family matters. In 1550, Menno Simons would not apply the ban to a woman who refused to abstain from sexual intercourse with her lapsed husband.[17] Six years later, while still calling the ban a "work of love," he became convinced that even marital avoidance was necessary when the ban was in operation.[18]

While the ban helped stabilize Radical Reformation congregations and earned most of them a reputation for decency, integrity, and morality, it also created schism and caused withdrawal in certain instances. Nevertheless, the Radical Reformation insisted on maintaining "quality control" over the church's life. Believers' baptism and the ban were the means by which church leadership attempted this.

A Distinctive View of Jesus Christ

Most of the radical reformers maintained a surprisingly high doctrine of Christ. This they drew mainly from our Lord's declaration in John 6:51: "I am the living bread that came down from heaven. Whoever eats of this bread will live forever; and the bread that I will give for the life of the world is my flesh." The doctrine of the "celestial flesh of Christ," based primarily on this verse, meant that when our Lord was incarnated by the Holy Spirit, he brought his own body with him from heaven.[19] This body was unlike any other human body, for if Christ had taken upon himself human flesh from his mother, how could Christ have been the Savior of the world?

Medieval thinking that assumed pearls formed from dew descending from heaven and crystallizing in an oyster influenced radical reformer Melchior Hofmann. He used this example to explain how the heavenly flesh of Christ came to earth to be solidified in the womb of the Virgin Mary. "The Eternal Word, which was true heavenly dew, in an unsensual and incomprehensible way but through the Holy

Spirit, fell from the mouth of God into the wild mussel of the Virgin Mary and in her became a bodily Word and spiritual pearl."[20] Thus our Lord was born out of, but not of, the Virgin Mary. Hofmann insisted that Jesus took nothing of substance from his earthly mother, but only passed through her "as water through a pipe."[21]

Both Roman Catholic and other Protestant theologians maligned the radical reformers for this doctrine, which departed from the definitive formula of the Council of Chalcedon of 451. The Council insisted that our Lord is one person with two natures, human and divine. John Calvin, for example, insisted that the Incarnation involved our Lord's genuine sharing of human nature, while at the same time the Holy Spirit sanctified him.[22]

This stress on Christ as unstained by human nature notwithstanding, the radical reformers understood the Christian life to be the imitation of Christ. Christian living involved following in our Lord's steps. Dietrich Philips wrote persuasively, "In all this the Lord Jesus Christ is to his own a master sent of God, whom they must hear (Matt. 3:17; 17:5); a leader (Voorganger) whom they must follow (1 Pet. 2:25); an example to which they must conform (Rom. 8:29)."[23]

A brief perusal of the Anabaptists' Schleitheim Confession of Faith of 1527 reveals how the basic ethical principles of the radical reformers had their source in the imitation of Christ. In effect, it stated that Christ was meek and lowly of heart ("We cannot, therefore, justify the use of the sword—even in self-defense"); Christ refused to pass judgment between two contesting brothers ("We, therefore, do not have recourse to a court of law"); Christ fled those who wanted to make him king ("We, therefore, cannot participate in government"); Christ prohibited all swearing of oaths ("We, therefore, refuse to take oaths to tell the truth when our speech already is an honest 'yes' or 'no'").[24]

Interestingly, the radical reformers' serious intent to live the Christian life as their Lord and Master had done caused them to look with some disdain on other Christians with lesser ethical standards. Conrad Grebel in 1524 criticized Zwingli and his clergy colleagues for preaching a "sinful, sweet Christ."[25] By contrast, certain radical reformers openly stressed the "bitter Christ," the life of suffering and possible martyrdom for those who took the imitation of Christ seriously.[26]

Not all those involved in the Radical Reformation lived up to such high ideals, including some of the leaders. Occasionally there were apostates and impostors. Certain Anabaptist groups advocated practices not in keeping with what the majority of their fellow believers held Christ's teachings to be. The vast number, however, sought to imitate Christ by not counting the cost. Most of them would have agreed with Pilgram Marpeck's interpretation of Colossians 1:24 that the suffering of the faithful for one another and for Christ in some way completes our Lord's suffering.[27]

The Great Commission

Adherents of the Radical Reformation had a keen sense of mission. They believed themselves to be the restitution of the "true Apostolic Church" and forerunners of the time to come when Christ would establish his people on earth. Their obedience to the Great Commission (Matt. 28:19–20) is evident in the preaching and travels of their courageous leaders. Hans Hut, for example, reportedly baptized thousands, telling them to obey the commandments and share the gospel under the mandate of the Great Commission.[28] He interpreted the missionary task of going into all the world to preach the gospel to include communicating the message of God's grace to common people through the use of parables and analogies from various crafts and occupations. "Jesus taught the gospel to the gardener by using the trees, to the fisherman by using the catch of fish, to the carpenter by using the house, to the goldsmith by using the smelting of gold—Matthew 13; Luke 13; 1 Corinthians 5; Galatians 5."[29] Hut appealed to all believers to witness for Christ. His advocacy of the use of simple language obviously included unschooled persons in the missionary task.

Here again, the radical reformers distanced themselves from the magisterial Reformation. The latter, in most instances, considered the Great Commission to be a command already obeyed by the apostles and not something sixteenth-century churches need follow. The radicals were not impressed in the least with the established church. Believing that they preached a saving word not being offered in the Roman mass or in Protestant state-church sermons, they went everywhere preaching and sharing, secretly and openly. The gentleness and courage of the vast majority of them lent integrity to their beliefs. Persecution forced them to migrate or flee and thus further spread their witness. Indeed, the Anabaptists were "among the first to make the Commission binding on all church members."[30]

THE ANABAPTIST SEGMENT

The Radical Reformation is usually divided into three groups: the Evangelical Anabaptists, the Spiritualists, and the Evangelical Rationalists. What distinguishes these three are the different basic authorities from which they drew.

The Evangelical Anabaptists used the holy scriptures as their basic authority. Their descendants in our day are the Mennonites, the Hutterites, and the Amish.

The Spiritualists were so named because they paid greater heed to what they perceived to be the direct revelation of the Holy Spirit, even above the authority of the holy scriptures. Although a number of leaders of this persuasion surfaced in the sixteenth century, only one of them, Caspar von Schwenkfeld, a German nobleman who surrendered everything to pursue mysticism, left a continuing organization as his legacy. The approximately twenty-seven hundred Schwenckfelders in the United States today are largely in Pennsylvania.

As their name implies, the Evangelical Rationalists were Protestants who gave speculative reason an authoritative place beside holy scripture. An uncle-and-nephew team, Lelio and Faustus Socinus of Siena, Italy, led in the rejection of such doctrines as the Trinity, the two natures of Christ, and original sin. Their considerable Polish Brethren following actually preferred to call themselves "Unitarian." They were driven from their native land. The Unitarian Universalist Association in the United States traces its heritage back to the Socinian movement.[31]

Swiss and South German Anabaptism

This study focuses upon the Anabaptist wing of the Radical Reformation and particularly those who are today known as the Mennonites.[32] We can best understand this group in terms of its geographical beginnings. In Zurich, Switzerland, and Southern Germany these people emerged under their preferred name of "Swiss Brethren." Their early leader was Conrad Grebel of Zurich. In 1522 this well-educated but turbulent man joined Zwingli's movement, remaining with it only a year. Impatient with Zwingli's cautious reformation, Grebel gathered with several expriest friends: Felix Manz, Georg Blaurock, and Wilhelm Reublin. These young, aggressive leaders, wanting a church separated from the state, publicly challenged Zwingli concerning the timid nature of his reform efforts and his support of infant baptism. Forbidden by the city council to continue their Bible study groups, they met secretly in Zurich on January 21, 1525, and performed the first believers' baptisms. That completed their break with Zwingli's Reformation.

By Easter of 1525 the Anabaptists had baptized hundreds of people in the Canton of Zurich as confessing believers. At the nearby imperial town of Waldshut, Wilhelm Reublin baptized Dr. Balthasar Hubmaier and sixty of his parishioners on Easter Sunday. Shortly thereafter Hubmaier baptized three hundred more.[33]

Zwingli and the Zurich city council were reluctant to persecute the growing numbers of dissidents, who claimed to have a new relationship with Christ through the ministry of these preachers who called them to new birth and into a separatist church. At first the city council demanded registration of all births so that parents could be forced to submit their infants to baptism on pain of banishment. When that failed, the city council in November of 1526 passed the "drowning edict," invoking the death penalty upon Anabaptist preachers and those who listened to them.

Arrested for a second time, Manz was condemned to death and Blaurock (because he was not a Zurich citizen) was whipped and banished. On January 5, 1527, Manz, with his hands and legs roped together, was drowned in the Limmat River, becoming the first Protestant martyr to die at the hands of other Protestants. Grebel escaped a similar fate due to his death from the plague during exile. Blaurock baptized a large following in the Austrian Tyrol before he was arrested and burned at the stake in 1529.

The largely nonviolent beliefs and the martyrdom of several of its significant leaders marked the spread of the Swiss and South German Anabaptist movement. Balthasar Hubmaier's doctorate in theology made him the best-educated Anabaptist leader. After 1526 he was active in Moravia, baptizing some six thousand followers and authoring seventeen publications before his death at the stake in 1528 in Vienna.

Jacob Hutter, a Tyrolean hat-maker, at least partially overcame division among Hubmaier's bereft followers when he united them through his preaching of resignation to the will of God, understood largely in terms of communal ownership of all possessions. Hutter was burned at the stake at Innsbruck in 1536. In the Black Forest area of Southwestern Germany, Michael Sattler, a former priest and prior of a Benedictine cloister, authored the Schleitheim Confession, adopted at a secret Anabaptist meeting in the Swiss town by that name in February 1527. This seven-article statement of faith was the oldest confession of nonviolent Anabaptism. It differentiated those people from the Protestant state churches and also from an increasing number of militant Anabaptists. The peace-loving Sattler was captured and burned at the stake at Rottenburg in the Black Forest in 1527. It should be noted that Elizabeth Hubmaier, Catharine Hutter, and Margaretha Sattler all faithfully followed their husbands in experiencing martyrs' deaths.

Anabaptism in the North

Not all Anabaptists were pacifists. Some from the very beginning advocated the use of the sword to restore the pure church of the past. More impressed with Old Testament imagery than their nonviolent cousins, these revolutionary Anabaptists envisioned the creation of a new Jerusalem on earth.[34]

An early herald of this more fanatical renewal style was Melchior Hofmann, a South German furrier. Devout and biblically knowledgeable, Hofmann between 1523 and 1529 served as a powerful Lutheran lay preacher in North Germany and Scandinavia. Upon becoming an Anabaptist in Strassburg in 1530, he introduced his new beliefs in Holland, winning many converts who took the name of "Melchiorites." Hofmann's studies in the Book of Revelation convinced him of Christ's imminent return. He predicted that the last judgment would occur in Strassburg in 1533. From there, 144,000 righteous ones would spread the true gospel throughout the world. After a successful preaching trip down the Rhine, Hofmann returned to Strassburg. He dared the officials there to arrest him, thinking that this would hasten Christ's return. Christ did not return as Hofmann prophesied, and he spent the last ten years of his life in a Strassburg prison.

Hofmann had not advised the faithful to take up the sword when Christ returned, but his militant preaching and his call to the pious magistrates in the free imperial cities to "seize the sword of vengeance and exterminate the godless"[35] injected a radical, revolutionary spirit into the Melchiorites. An example of Melchiorite excess occurred in early 1535 when seven men and five women stripped off all their clothes as a sign of their speaking the naked truth and ran through the streets of Amsterdam, crying "Woe! Woe! Woe! The wrath of God!" Their immediate capture and execution intensified the cruel persecution of the Anabaptists.[36]

Leading the Dutch Melchiorites at that time was Jan Matthys, a Haarlem baker, who was in the process of gathering "twelve apostles" to assist him. One of these was Jan Bockelson, a Leiden tailor. Under their opportunistic and unbalanced leadership, the Melchiorites increased in number and radical commitment. Beleaguered by persecution, they welcomed the news that their movement could find asylum in the city of Münster in Northwest Germany. With Hofmann's prophecies unfulfilled, Matthys and Bockelson proclaimed Münster instead of Strassburg the New Jerusalem.

Although hundreds of Melchiorites lost their lives attempting to reach Münster, many others arrived there. Matthys and Bockelson were on hand by early 1534. Aided by the large number of radical refugees, they gained mastery over the city. Those who resisted being baptized or surrendering their property were banished. This itself was dangerous because the local Roman Catholic bishop besieged the city with an army of Roman Catholic and Lutheran troops.

Only tragedy ensued. In a fanatic display of courage Matthys sallied forth in April 1534 with just twenty men to lift the siege. They were all killed. Bockelson, who now proclaimed himself "King David," began arbitrary rule. He introduced polygamy in July of that year, setting the example by taking sixteen wives, including Matthys's widow. An internal rebellion was suppressed bloodily. The besieged radicals cultivated every available plot of ground in order to avoid starvation.

The Münster episode ended on June 24, 1535, when the bishops' forces captured the city. Every Anabaptist man still bearing arms was put to the sword. Bockelson's wife, "Queen Divara," and others of his harem were beheaded. Captured unwounded, Bockelson was led from town to town between two horsemen holding a double chain about his neck. Six months later, he and other radical leaders were tortured to death. Their bodies were hung upside down in iron cages placed in the tower of St. Lambert's Church in downtown Münster. The cages hang there to this day.[37]

A majority of Europeans were relieved that this cancer in the body politic had been removed. For the Roman Catholics and magisterial Protestants, Münster represented what Jonestown in 1978 and the Branch Davidians of Waco, Texas, in 1993 did for most contemporary North Americans. Unfortunately, many formed unfair judgments that confused the Münster revolutionary Anabaptists with the peaceful Anabaptist majority. Such attitudes led to increased efforts to stamp out Anabaptism by sword and fire. This reaction explains all the more the invaluable service rendered by Menno Simons. He and the other Evangelical Anabaptist leaders risked their lives and reputations in order to teach and discipline their followers so that with integrity they could present them to the wider, hostile society as a community of decency, honesty, industry, and nonviolence.

THE LIFE STORY OF MENNO SIMONS

The most significant Anabaptist leader was Menno Simons (1496–1561), a Dutch dairy farmer's son. He probably received his education at the Franciscan monastery at Bolsward in the Netherlands. He learned to read and write Latin rather well, could read Greek, and was acquainted with the writings of several of the church fathers. Ordained a Roman Catholic priest in 1524, he served parishes at Pingjim and Witmarsum, his hometown near the North Sea. Two years after his ordination, Menno first read the holy scriptures.[38]

Menno admitted that in his first years as a priest he carelessly performed his parish duties. He gave himself to card playing, gluttony, and drinking. He wrote, "I was like a beautifully whitewashed crypt. On the outside, before others, I looked moral, chaste, and serene. Nobody found fault with my conduct. But on the inside I was nothing but dead bones, stinking flesh, and gnawing worms. On the outside, my cup was clean, but on the inside it was full of plunder and indulgence."[39]

This all began to change, however. Diligent reading of the New Testament and Luther left Simons doubting the doctrine of transubstantiation. For a time he suppressed his doubts and continued to be a popular priest. He remembered, "Everyone sought and desired me; the world loved me and I loved the world. It was said that I preached the Word of God and was a good fellow."[40]

The practice of infant baptism and the persecution of those who objected to it helped to thrust Menno out of his comfortable parish position. When Sicke Snijder, a God-fearing, pious man, was beheaded for having been rebaptized, Simons began to read the New Testament all the more diligently, finding to his satisfaction no warrant for infant baptism. Reading Luther and other reformers on this topic failed to dissuade him.

Menno quietly considered but did not yet express his inner convictions regarding the sacraments. He tried to be an evangelical preacher in a Roman Catholic pulpit. His condemnation of the excesses of the Münsterites earned him praise. Then in March 1535 another tragedy finalized his decision to leave the Roman Catholic priesthood. About three hundred revolutionary Anabaptists, including his own brother, barricaded themselves in a nearby monastery. They were all killed when the monastery was captured. Although he disagreed with their violent measures, Simons felt guilty that he had shared with some of them his own misgivings about Rome and yet lacked the courage of their convictions.

Under these circumstances Menno experienced conversion that was more than a change of denominational loyalty. He wrote:

> My heart trembled within me. I prayed to God with sighs and tears that He would give to me, a sorrowing sinner, the gift of His grace, create within me a clean heart, and graciously through the merits of the crimson blood of Christ forgive my unclean walk and frivolous easy life and bestow upon me wisdom, Spirit, courage and a manly spirit so that I might preach His exalted and adorable name and holy Word in purity and make known His truth to His glory. And so . . . the merciful Lord through the liberal goodness of His

abounding grace took notice of me, a poor sinner, stirred in my heart at the outset, produced in me a new mind, humbled me in His fear, taught me to know myself in part, turned me from the way of death and graciously called me into the narrow pathway of life and the communion of His saints. To Him be praise forevermore. Amen.[41]

Menno's words aptly described not only the spiritual transition he had experienced within himself but also the new way of life he was about to enter. On January 30, 1536, he resigned from the priesthood. Casting his lot with the Evangelical and nonrevolutionary Anabaptists, he was rebaptized. In 1537 he was reordained. About that same time he married a woman known only as Gertrude. Their twenty-year marriage ended at her death. Only one of their three children survived their father.

For seven years Menno ministered to Anabaptist people in his native Holland. He traveled from place to place, meeting secretly with little groups of Anabaptists. His pastoral problems were immense. Obbe Philips, the Evangelical Anabaptist leader who had probably ordained Menno, forsook the movement. Another colleague, David Joris, departed from an orthodox biblical position and began teaching that his own writings (which he claimed were inspired) were a higher revelation of God than holy scripture. Joris enticed followers by offering an easy morality. He said that Christians should confess sin until they no longer felt a sense of shame for it.[42] Menno published openly against him. In fact, he wrote three books during his Holland ministry.

Menno's success in stabilizing the growing number of Evangelical Anabaptist congregations in Holland came to the attention of the authorities, who sought in vain to bribe his followers to betray him. Ultimately, they persuaded Emperor Charles V to issue an edict against

Menno, which placed a sizeable price on his head and forbade reading his books or sheltering him in any way. Menno, undeterred, carried on his ministry in Amsterdam for two more years. When some of his followers paid with their lives for harboring him, however, Menno left Holland for good in 1543. The emperor's edict would have less effect in the German lands that were rapidly falling under Lutheran control.[43]

For the rest of his life Menno ministered in Northwest Germany, itinerating among the scattered, discouraged, sometimes misled, and frequently persecuted Evangelical Anabaptist congregations. These met secretly in the woods, barns, and private homes. He became the chief elder or bishop of the growing number of people who accepted his teaching and took his name. Menno appears to have been crippled by a stroke the last years of his life.[44] Thanks to Bartholomaus von Ahlefeldt, a nobleman in Holstein, who made his lands a refuge for persecuted Anabaptists, Menno was able to die peacefully in his own bed in Wüstenfelde, a village between Hamburg and Lübeck.[45]

It is ironic that Menno, whose direct influence was limited to Holland and North Germany and who even shortly before his death excommunicated all the Swiss/South German Anabaptists, should have given his name to the descendants of these people who live in North America today.[46] He did not even found the church which bears his name. It began in Zurich, Switzerland, eleven years before he joined it.[47]

A born leader, Menno Simons made a stellar contribution to the Evangelical Anabaptists who took his name. His influence was twofold. First, he gathered his persecuted Dutch and German followers into organized congregations. He traveled effectively among them as a general superintendent, offering to help local elders and to strengthen congregations as they faced moral and theological tensions within or hostile governments without.[48] He also sought to persuade the governing authorities that these law-abiding, pacifist people had no connection with the revolutionary Anabaptists who constituted a violent threat to Roman Catholic and Protestant state churches.

Second, Menno's twenty-five books and tracts, as well as his letters and hymns, provided a body of literature around which Evangelical Anabaptists could rally. In our time these have been gathered by John C. Wenger into *The Complete Works of Menno Simons,* a collection of more than a thousand pages. Included in this volume is Menno's most influential work, *The Foundation of Christian Doctrine,* first published in 1540.

Menno was not a profound thinker or literary stylist. Nevertheless, with his strong faith, pastoral concern, and personal integrity, he communicated effectively with the peasants, manual laborers, and shopkeepers who, by and large, constituted his following. In order to emphasize the Christ-centered faith to which he beckoned them, he placed on the title page of each of his publications, "For no one can lay any foundation other than the one that has been laid; that foundation is Jesus Christ" (1 Cor. 3:11).

MENNO'S UNDERSTANDING
OF THE CHRISTIAN FAITH

Two main themes of Menno's writings and ministry are the doctrine of the New Birth, or regeneration, and his doctrine of the church.[49] The New Birth and resultant new life in Christ were of paramount importance to the Anabaptist leader. His own conversion was an experience of the new birth in Christ. He put it plainly:

> O poor, blind men, be silent and shamed. Let Christ Jesus with His Spirit and Word be your teacher and example, your way and your mirror. Do you think that it is enough merely to acknowledge Christ according to the flesh, or to

say that you believe on Him, that you are baptized, that you are Christian, that you are purchased with the blood and death of Christ? Ah, no! I have told you often and tell you once more, you must be so born of God. In your life you must be so converted and changed that you become new men in Christ, so that Christ is in you and you are in Christ. Otherwise you can never be Christians, for, "If any man be in Christ, he is a new creature" (2 Cor. 5:17).[50]

Both his reading of the New Testament and his own personal religious experience established the necessity of the New Birth for Menno. It was only by this means that Christians could become the changed persons they were meant to be.

Paralleling Menno's writings regarding the New Birth was his understanding of the church. Because Christians as individuals are new creatures in Christ, the church, a voluntary association made up of such people, should have a new and redeemed look. Menno listed six signs that would identify the true church. The first was the saving and unadulterated doctrine of God's holy and divine word. This meant that the pure and right preaching of the word of God was a sure indicator of the church's presence. Second, "right and Scriptural use of the sacraments" denoted the church. This meant, for Menno, baptism of those who are born again in the faith and those who come to the Lord's Table in true penitence and expectation. Third was obedience to the holy word or a pious Christian life. Christian holiness was an expectation. Fourth was "the sincere and unfeigned love of one's neighbor." Fifth was the confession of the name, will, word, and ordinance of Christ "in the face of all cruelty, tyranny, tumult, fire, sword, and violence of the world and sustained to the end." This obviously referred to the "suffering church," which both Menno's doctrine and experience informed him to be the norm. Last was "the pressing cross of Christ," a corollary to Menno's fifth point. Christians have to expect suffering and persecution. In it they are admonished to be cheerful and patient.

With each sign of the true church, Menno provided the marks of the false and hypocritical one. Infant baptism was the root cause of all that was wrong in the "church of anti-Christ" because its very low admission standards made it possible for hateful, deceitful, faithless, avaricious, murderous, profane, and licentious people to affirm that they were Christians and respectable church members.[51]

Menno located the true church of God only in the broken, scattered, and persecuted Anabaptist congregations of his time. The church is "an assembly of the pious and a community of the saints."[52] He even contended that "it is sufficiently proved that our hated, despised, and small church is the true, prophetic, apostolic, and Christian church."[53]

Nevertheless, Menno stopped shy of affirming the doctrine of Christian perfection and applying it to the Anabaptist congregations. He avoided this by stating that Christians may commit transgressions—but not willingly. Their frailties may reveal themselves in careless thoughts or words or unpremeditated lapses in conduct. These would not amount to willful and major transgressions, however.[54] Of course, Christians were to live up to the high maxims found in the Sermon on the Mount. It is clear why the radicals had to employ believers' baptism and the ban to keep the church as pure as possible. Of course, not all Christians then or now would agree with the separatist, quasilegalistic, and sectarian view of the church that Menno and his followers upheld.

Menno Simons's life and ministry testify to his high understanding of the church. He spent his dangerous twenty-five-year ministry attempting to edify the body of Christ. When he held debates with highly individualistic Anabaptist leaders and published against them, he did so to maintain the corporate nature of the Christian life. He had harsh words for rival Anabaptist leaders who threatened the unity and peace of the church.

MENNO'S INSIGHTS FOR CHRISTIAN LIVING

Menno Simons made several important contributions to an understanding of the Christian life, one being his emphasis on the significance of Christian suffering. Basing his arguments upon the scriptural accounts of how God's faithful have suffered, as well as recounting the torment experienced by so many Evangelical Anabaptists in his own time, he openly called upon his fellow believers to take up the cross. A refugee in frequent danger himself, he personally possessed the credentials for issuing such a challenge.

Menno was not above castigating Roman Catholic and Protestant persecutors, who with their "poor, blind, hardened hearts" did not perceive the spirit of true Christians. Could they do so, they would be ashamed of the wickedness they were committing against Christ and his word: "Christ Jesus does not recognize such wanton, carnal, frightful, and bloodthirsty Christians. He knows only those that have His Spirit."[55] The anguished cry of a wounded and maligned leader understandably resounds in these defensive words.

For all that, Menno upheld the blessings of suffering. Because our weak and sinful human nature has a tendency to heed earthly and perishable things, the gracious Father has left an excellent remedy for all this: "the pressing cross of Christ."[56] Menno was satisfied that those who suffered for the sake of the will and word of God were not likely to give in to the false attractions of earthly ease, peace, and prosperity.

True Christians would be more attuned to things of the Holy Spirit.

Menno acknowledged that the call to cross bearing for Christ's sake was costly but worthwhile:

> We know very well, dear brethren, how that this cross seems to the flesh grievous, harsh, and severe, and in the present is not considered a matter of joy, but rather of sorrow, even as Paul says. But since it contains within itself so much of profit and delight, in that it constantly adds to the piety of the pious, turns them away from the world and the flesh, makes them revere God and His Word . . . and since it is also the Father's holy will that by it the saints should be approved, and the pretender exposed in his hypocrisy, therefore all the true children of God are prepared to love, to do the will of the Father, rejoicing in it.[57]

Many Christians in our day might reject Menno's insistence that joy and value are inherent in suffering. We can be grateful that in the United States of America, at least, Christians live under a government committed to guaranteeing freedom of religion. The problem of human suffering and its place within the will of God is far too vast to discuss here. What is necessary, however, is to acknowledge that Menno Simons, in addressing the issue of Christian cross bearing, recognized outright the pain it involved. He further illustrated the biblical and historical precedent for it and the positive effect it could have upon faithful souls who embraced rather than resisted it. In addition he emphasized biblical promises that God's grace would attend those made miserable for their faith's sake all the way up to and including physical death.

Another contribution to our understanding of Christian living was Menno Simons's insistence upon the manner in which the New

Birth creates new people. He was not overly specific as to how the New Birth came about. Of course, it originated from the proclamation of the word of the Lord. A believer received it in true repentance. It resulted in newness of life and eternal salvation. What was important for Menno was the change the New Birth made in peoples' lives. As he said,

> The regenerate, therefore, lead a penitent and new life, for they are renewed in Christ and have received a new heart and spirit. Once they were earthly-minded, now heavenly; once they were carnal, now spiritual; once they were unrighteous, now righteous; once they were evil, now good, and they live no longer after the old corrupted nature of the first earthly Adam, but after the new upright nature of the new and heavenly Adam, Christ Jesus, even as Paul says, "Nevertheless, I live; yet not I, but Christ liveth in me."[58]

It may well be that Menno occasionally claimed too much for his followers, but he clearly recognized that Christians are to be "a breed apart." They are persons ostensibly with a renewed nature, a deeper perception, a caring posture, a unique orientation, and eternal goals. Despite abiding weaknesses (which Menno estimated were of lesser gravity than manifest public sins), Christians are, as our Lord expected, salt and light in the world. Even if Menno himself seemed to be a somber and serious mentor and a leader "who ran a tight ship," he aptly described the high ground he expected his followers to occupy.

One final contribution Menno Simons makes to our understanding of the Christian life yet today is his exemplary life. He had the courage of his convictions. He dared to oppose openly and in print those Anabaptist leaders who were, in his judgment, causing havoc in his loose-knit confederation of congregations. He did this, never knowing when one or more of these people might vengefully betray him to his state church enemies. They never did.

Menno labored without the comparable securities that the magisterial reformers enjoyed. His principle of separation of church and state automatically precluded his receiving either a guaranteed security or salary from the state church. He referred to himself as a "homeless man."[59] The simple cottage in the insignificant village in which he spent his last years was his only by the grace of a nobleman, who was personally disgusted with the injustices done to the Anabaptists.

Menno was also a poor man. His writings and his ministry earned him little financial support. The humble and simple manner of life he led was likely from necessity as well as from choice.

Menno Simons was perhaps no more courageous than Luther, who stood alone at Worms, uncertain of the outcome of his bold defense. We must also recall that Zwingli died for his cause on the battlefield and Calvin bared his breast to his vicious enemies at a Geneva city council meeting. Menno, like they, demonstrated that the flip side of integrity is a bravery that does not flinch from taking risks. He traveled through hostile territory to visit and encourage his followers. He met dangers from without and divisions from within his constituency. An appreciative scholar in our century wrote, "Humble and self-effacing to the end, Simons's greatest contribution to the Anabaptist movement was his character."[60]

A PRAYER OF MENNO SIMONS

Ah, faithful Father, Lord,

My flesh has strength no more,

This earthly house Thou breakest sore.

The vile world hates me quite,

For this Thy witness bright;

Thy cross I bear, with grief not light.

And yet—adversity!

Thy hand Thou lay'st on me,

And presses so

My flesh lays low!

Yet rest I me

Upon Thy promise free

Which ever sure shall be;

And praise Thy majesty

In all eternity![61]

FOR PERSONAL OR GROUP REFLECTION

1. What sentiments arise within you as you read the brief accounts of martyrdom of Elizabeth Dirks, Dirk Willems, and Hans Bret?

2. Most Anabaptist groups desired a pure church. They used believers' baptism to control admission to the church and the ban to discipline those who were admitted. What do you believe are the marks of true discipleship? How should these marks impact church membership today?

3. Were you baptized as an infant or as a believer? What do you see as the significance of infant baptism? of believers' baptism?

4. Some of the Anabaptists attacked the magisterial reformers for preaching a "sinful, sweet Christ" (a Christ who graciously forgives people in their sins). These Anabaptist preachers preferred to stress the "bitter Christ" (a Christ who forgives but also makes radical demands of his followers). How do you react to this comparison? From whom do you think the church in our day needs to hear more?

5. Virtually all the Evangelical Anabaptists were pacifists. They believed that the sword was acceptable for the government's use because the government was "outside the perfection of Christ." The Anabaptist congregations, which constituted the "perfection of Christ," could use only the ban as a weapon. How do you feel about pacifism or the use of violence?

6. What most impressed you about the life story of Menno Simons?

7. Relate how you felt when you first read Menno Simons's account of his conversion. Has your faith journey included such an experience? Do all people need to come to Christ over a route similar to this? Why or why not?

8. In their book, *On Fire for Christ: Stories of Anabaptist Martyrs Retold from Martyrs Mirror,* Dave and Neta Jackson say of the martyrs, "Their goal was not to stay alive—as ours might have been. Their goal was to make a good witness, to die faithfully. To have that opportunity was deemed a privilege. The greatest tragedy would have been to save their life just to have it fade away in secure old age" (p. 12). The word *martyr* comes from a Greek root meaning "witness." Do you think the Anabaptist martyrs made the witness they desired to make? Where do you see people willing to die for the Christian faith today?

THOMAS CRANMER

CHAPTER 5

A Prayer Book to Reform the Church

THE LIFE AND MINISTRY
OF THOMAS CRANMER

---

*E*nglish adults living between 1530 and 1560 had to be flexible indeed in order to endure the religious changes that swept across them under four monarchs. Serious Roman Catholics and Protestants paid the ultimate price for their resistance to them. The vast majority, however, apparently imitated the Elizabethan bishop who had survived each regime. When asked how he did it, he replied, "I smacked of the willow more than of the oak."[1] With willowy perseverance or perhaps what they blithely call "muddling through," the island nation of England finally avoided extreme solutions to the pressing religious questions of the sixteenth century.

Two interesting facts about the Reformation in England demand notation at the outset. First of all, it was accomplished primarily as an act of state.[2] Rather than a popular movement aroused by the preaching and publications of a noteworthy leader, the Reformation was legislated by Parliament under royal pressure. Second and no less important, England was "the largest and most important political unit to secede at one blow from Catholic

Christendom."[3] As such, it helped assure a permanent Protestant presence on the continent.

The seeds of the English Reformation had been planted long before. In the fourteenth century the prereformer, John Wyclif, had aroused an antipapal mood. Parliament responded with legislation limiting the pope's prerogatives. By the sixteenth century the English people, although conservative by nature and desiring no theological changes, were expressing discontent with the church locally. There was resentment that one-third of the land in England belonged to the church; that farmers had to pay a tithe to the church alongside the clerical fees for baptisms, weddings, and funerals; and that clergy who committed crimes received much lighter penalties in the church courts they were tried in than laypersons would receive for the same offenses in the civil courts.

English Christian humanists like Thomas More and John Colet added to the anticlergy mood by attacking the ignorance of parish priests and the worldliness of many bishops. Some of the rural monasteries no longer commanded the high respect they had once received.[4]

This was the situation in the 1520s when at Cambridge University a group of scholars began reading Luther's works with approval. Their meetings at the White Horse Tavern were dubbed "Little Germany." The transfer of some of these professors to a new college at Oxford University inadvertently spread Protestant ideas.

THE INFLUENCE OF ENGLISH MONARCHS ON THE REFORMATION

The Anglican Reformation took various turns during the reigns of the last four persons of the House of Tudor to sit on England's throne.

Henry VIII: Ruler from 1509–47

The break with Rome actually came about through a secondary but well-known issue. King Henry VIII, lacking a male heir and wanting to marry Anne Boleyn, sought a divorce from his Spanish wife, Catherine of Aragon. When the papacy for political reasons refused Henry's request, his legislation rammed through Parliament between 1532 and 1534 effectively severed England from Rome. The Act of Supremacy declared the king and his successors "the only supreme head in earth of the Church of England." The Act of Succession sanctioned the divorce and granted the king the option of demanding a loyalty oath of his subjects. The church in England had now become the Church of England.

Henry VIII demonstrated his arbitrary but legal powers by executing a number of loyal Roman Catholics who refused the loyalty oath. His closing of the monasteries all over England and confiscation of their lands dealt the Roman Catholic church a devastating blow. Henry ruled powerfully, if not always justly. He is well known for his succession of six wives and for his three children, all of whom succeeded him on the British throne.[5] Never really a Protestant, he left England Catholic but antipapal.

Edward VI: Ruler from 1547–53

Edward VI, Henry's son by Jane Seymour, succeeded him. Edward was nine when he ascended the throne. During his six-year "reign," a privy council of advisors to the king, headed initially by Edward Seymour (the Duke of Somerset), Edward's uncle, actually ruled England.

The Seymour family was Protestant, and during the reign of the ailing but studious boy-king, Protestantism made great gains in

England. Parliament made it law that laypeople receive the cup along with the bread in the Lord's Supper. The issuance in 1549 of the first prayer book in the English language led to strong criticism from both Roman Catholics and Protestants who found it to be either too radical or not radical enough.

Under other leadership a second prayer book and a creed of some forty-two articles were issued. The latter was anti-Roman Catholic and also anti-Anabaptist. The accession of Edward's half-sister, Mary, to the throne upon his death in 1553 rendered these both inoperative.

Mary Tudor: Ruler from 1553–58

Mary Tudor was Henry VIII's daughter by Catherine of Aragon. She was intelligent, schooled in several languages, serious by nature, and a devout Roman Catholic. As much as a princess could, she resisted Henry VIII's breaking England away from the pope in Rome. She assumed the throne after having quelled a Protestant and political coup intended to keep her from it.

Advised by her cousin, Emperor Charles V, Mary appeared magnanimous at first in dealing with Protestants, executing only the coup leaders. She soon had the Roman mass restored to all English churches and deprived all married priests of their parishes. Soon after, about eight hundred Protestant preachers and laity fled to the safety of the continent. They were called the "Marian Exiles." Mary also arrested the leading Protestant bishops.

Mary's 1554 marriage to King Philip II of Spain and the fact that she was half-Spanish did not endear her to her subjects. Even more they resented her persecution of the Protestants, whom she hated. Beginning in February 1555, some three hundred people were executed during her short reign for not accepting the reestablishment of Roman Catholicism. A vast majority of these perished in the "Smithfield Fires" near London. Archbishop Thomas Cranmer and Bishops John Hooper, Hugh Latimer, and Nicholas Ridley were all burned at the stake. Labeled "Bloody Mary," the English queen ultimately failed in her pro-Roman Catholic and anti-Protestant efforts. She died of cancer. Her inflexibility caused her only defeat and heartache.

The publication of John Foxe's *Acts and Monuments of Matters Happening in the Church* (commonly referred to as *The Book of Martyrs)* drove Mary's sorrowful legacy deep into the consciousness of those she ruled. A committed Calvinist, Foxe provided well-researched if somewhat dramatic accounts of Protestants who died for their beliefs during Mary's persecution. By writing in English instead of Latin, Foxe was able to reach the widest audience possible. For more than a century in English Protestant homes only the English Bible exceeded *The Book of Martyrs* in influence.

Elizabeth I: Ruler from 1558–1603

The last Tudor monarch to rule England was Mary's half-sister, Elizabeth, daughter of Henry VIII and Ann Boleyn. A true offspring of both her parents, she was cunning, bold, intelligent, an able scholar and horsewoman, vain, impetuous, and passionate. She was well endowed with the gifts of diplomacy and managerial skills. Her aim was to preserve England and herself as England's queen. So well did she succeed at this during her forty-five-year reign that her subjects lovingly called her "Good Queen Bess."

The resolution of the religious question that came about has been referred to as "The Elizabethan Settlement." Parliament passed a new Supremacy Act that made Elizabeth not the "supreme head of the church" (that is Christ alone) but the church's "supreme governor." It pointedly insisted that no foreign prince or bishop should have any jurisdiction over the English church. The Act of Uniformity of that same year, 1559, ordered the worship life of the nation. Trying to appeal to the vast majority of English people who remained in the middle between the conservative Roman Catholic wing and the growing liberal Puritan party, Elizabeth announced that while she "would not make windows into mens' hearts," she would control their bodies in worship.[6] She accomplished this by reissuing the *Book of Common Prayer* of 1552, now somewhat moderated so as not to offend Roman Catholics. The laity received both the bread and wine in the liturgy, which was restored to the English language. The words of administration of the bread and wine could be interpreted from a moderate Catholic or a Protestant perspective.

In 1563 the Thirty-nine Articles of the Church of England were adopted. This creedal statement contained a basically Protestant faith stance with some acknowledgment of Roman Catholic theology as well.

Elizabeth desired a broad national and episcopal church in which moderate Catholics and Protestants could find their spiritual home. Two men helped her achieve this goal: William Cecil (Lord Burghley), her chief political advisor, and Matthew Parker, whom she made Archbishop of Canterbury in 1559. Their wise advice on matters political and religious helped the gifted Elizabeth to steady the course and survive several difficult crises. The vast majority of her subjects were content with Elizabeth's melding of traditional and new elements into a church once described as "Protestant without being evangelical and Catholic without being Roman."[7]

In addition to Foxe's martyrology, the Reformation in England distinguished itself with the production of two even more important books. The first of these was a succession of English translations of holy scripture. The second was its *Book of Common Prayer*. Both had far-reaching influence beyond the Anglican Church (the Church of England) in the wider English-speaking Protestant world. William Tyndale was responsible for the first and Thomas Cranmer, the second. Although Cranmer was the major reforming influence, a brief history of William Tyndale is due for his contribution as well.

THE INFLUENCE OF WILLIAM TYNDALE
(C. 1494–1536)

William Tyndale was born into an English family living near the Welsh border. By 1515 he had gained both his bachelor's and master's degrees at Oxford and in that year entered Cambridge. It was at Cambridge that he likely encountered Lutheran teachings, possibly by conversation with the German reformer's disciples at the White Horse Tavern. He mastered seven languages: Hebrew, Greek, Latin, Italian, English, Spanish, and French.

In 1521 the rather severe Tyndale left Cambridge University, taking employment as a chaplain on a nobleman's estate near Bath. There he became keenly aware of the biblical illiteracy of the clergy who visited his benefactor. He told one of them that if God would spare his life, he would soon cause a boy that drives a plow to know more of scripture than the priest did.[8]

Refused assistance in England for his mission of providing a fresh English translation of the Bible from Greek and Hebrew texts, Tyndale went abroad. At Wittenberg he met Luther and studied for a time at the university.[9] At Worms in 1526 he published six thousand copies of his English New Testament.

Tyndale's decidedly Lutheran comments in the margins made his translation unwelcome in his native land. Therefore he smuggled the pages of his new translation into England in bales of wool.[10] England's Roman Catholic bishops were alarmed and required that all who owned copies of this new work surrender them to be burned.[11]

Tyndale planned to complete an Old Testament translation as well. Before undertaking that, however, he published in 1528 *The Obedience of the Christian Man*. He intended to refute the allegation that the new Protestantism would lead to rebellion and social fragmentation. So much did he champion the "divine right of kings" idea and counsel subjects to obey their rulers that King Henry VIII proclaimed, "This book is for me and all kings to read."[12]

Tyndale was a reformer as well as a Bible translator. In his *Parable of the Wicked Mammon* and *Obedience of the Christian Man* he affirmed justification by faith alone. His *Practice of Prelates* attacked the Roman Catholic hierarchy. By then in hiding in Antwerp, he translated the Pentateuch (the first five Old Testament books) in 1531. His biting criticisms let to his betrayal and arrest. When he was burned at the stake in 1536, Tyndale's last words were, "Lord, open the King of England's eyes."[13]

Tyndale's prayer eventually was answered. Already in Zurich in 1535, his disciple, Miles Coverdale, had published the first complete English Bible. It was heavily dependent upon Tyndale. In 1537 King Henry VIII permitted the translation of the entire Bible by John Rogers, another Tyndale disciple, to be published and sold throughout England.[14] Other translations would follow.

The fresh use of language and the high quality of Tyndale's translation is evident in the fact that an estimated 90 percent of his wording was later used in the King James Version of the Bible of 1611 and more than 75 percent in the Revised Standard Version of 1952.[15] Tyndale's placing of the holy scriptures into the language of laypersons was an invaluable contribution to the Reformation in England.

THE LIFE STORY OF THOMAS CRANMER
(1489–1556)

Thomas Cranmer was born in a Nottinghamshire village on July 2, 1489, into a gentleman's family consisting of three boys and four or five girls. The short but sturdy youth suffered under a cruel schoolmaster, but his kind father taught him to be an excellent horseman and hunter. Cranmer was twelve when his father died, but his mother saw to his education. At age fourteen he entered Jesus College at Cambridge University.

Cranmer in 1511 received his bachelor's degree. All studies were in Latin, but the future archbishop also learned Greek, Hebrew, and some of the modern languages. His proficiency in the latter came later when he was on the continent in the king's service.[16] Cranmer was something of a "plodder" as a student; he was more diligent than brilliant. He graduated thirty-second in a class of forty-two. He received his master's degree in 1514.[17] He left no record as to whether he heard the lectures of the famous Erasmus, who was teaching at Cambridge at that time.

Cranmer lost the fellowship that supported his studies by marrying, in 1515 or 1516, a young woman known only as "Black Joan of the Dolphin" (named for the Dolphin Inn, a tavern in Cambridge). This marriage was no crime as Cranmer was not ordained at the time. When Joan and her baby died in childbirth, Cranmer found some relief from his sorrow in his readmission as a fellow of Jesus College. Such an unusual restoration suggests the respect Cranmer had earned not only from his diligent studies but also the manly way in which he openly surrendered his future as a scholar in order to care for his wife and child.

At about the age of thirty, Cranmer was ordained a Roman Catholic priest. During this period he became convinced that it was far more important for clergy to give themselves to biblical studies than to philosophy. After he became a doctor of divinity in 1526, he endeavored to correct this situation among the university students for whom he was academically responsible.[18]

During the summer of 1529 a chance meeting occurred that thrust the respected but less-than-brilliant theologian onto the national stage. By that time, dinner conversation among England's middle and upper classes included discreet reference to "the king's business"—Henry VIII's desire to find a legal way out of his marriage to Catherine of Aragon. Cranmer was tutoring a nobleman's sons near Waltham when he encountered at dinner some former Cambridge colleagues now in the king's service. It was they who reported to the king a suggestion of Cranmer's: that instead of appealing to the pope for a divorce, Henry ought to obtain a hopefully affirmative judgment from the theologians at universities at home and abroad. The king received this advice enthusiastically. The modest professor, lacking vaulting ambition, soon found himself summoned by the king to a better-paying position.[19] He lived with the Boleyn family while he wrote his book supporting Henry VIII's position.

Henry VIII in 1530 sent Cranmer to Rome to represent his position on the divorce to the pope and also to Italian theologians. The next year found Cranmer representing his king at the court of Emperor Charles V in Germany. In November of 1532, during his stay at Nuremberg, Cranmer secretly married Margaret Osiander, the niece of the Lutheran reformer there. By forsaking clerical celibacy, he clearly announced his support for the Protestant Reformation. Imagine Cranmer's surprise when that same month he was recalled to England by the king to become the new Archbishop of Canterbury. Cranmer took an unusually long time in returning to London. He accepted the highest position in the English church with great reluctance.[20]

Although Pope Clement VII was suspicious of Cranmer's theology, for political reasons he confirmed Henry VIII's nominee to become the new primate of England. At his consecration on March 10, 1533, Cranmer took the oath that his predecessors in office had affirmed for four centuries—that they would place loyalty to the king above obedience to the pope.[21]

The Archbishop of Canterbury

It is not incorrect to label Thomas Cranmer "Henry VIII's Archbishop." The king chose him from among a number of persons, including a pool of able bishops, some of whom ardently desired the position. Not for three hundred years had the monarchy selected a nonbishop to occupy the archbishopric of Canterbury.[22] Henry named Cranmer to this post because he realized that the latter, seeking no personal gain for himself, would faithfully do the royal bidding. Cranmer took the job knowing that his imperious employer would sometimes demand his doing the distasteful. He reconciled himself to this with the solid conviction that "under God, he had a solemn obligation as archbishop to be obedient to the 'godly prince.'"[23] Indeed, in Cranmer's letters one frequently encounters the phrase "God and the King," which suggests that the archbishop somehow believed that in his position he could best serve God by carefully looking out for the interests of his king.[24]

Once consecrated, Cranmer complied with Henry's wishes. On May 23, 1533, he declared the twenty-four-year marriage between Henry VIII and Catherine of Aragon null and void. For reasons of royal succession, however, he declared that their daughter, Mary, was not illegitimate because her parents had acted in good faith! Five days later he declared Anne Boleyn Henry's lawful wife. On June 1, with great ceremony at Westminster Abbey, the archbishop crowned Anne, whom Henry had married secretly the previous December, Queen of England. For this, the pope excommunicated Henry, Anne, and Cranmer. Another papal bull deprived Cranmer of his archbishopric. Cranmer and his king now just ignored the pope. On September 3, 1533, Queen Anne gave birth to a daughter, Elizabeth.

Cranmer discovered that although he held considerable power as archbishop, he was also subject to intense criticism from the Roman Catholics in England as well as from the growing Protestant populace. Beyond that were times when he had to set conscience aside to serve the king. When Queen Anne was convicted of adultery and sent to the block in 1536, Cranmer wrote a letter to Henry telling of his love for the queen but not directly interceding for her. He wrote because the king refused him an audience. Cranmer did hear Anne Boleyn's last confession the day before she was beheaded. He also pronounced Henry's marriage to Anne Boleyn null and void.

When in that same year the crown took over all the monasteries, Cranmer did not object. He did let the king know, however, of his deep dissatisfaction over the way the king used the monastic properties to enrich the nobles instead of devoting them to the financing of hospitals and education.[25]

A genuine crisis emerged for Cranmer in 1540 when the conservative Roman Catholic party was able to turn Henry VIII against Thomas Cromwell (1485–1540), the king's able principal secretary and vice-regent. The latter and Cranmer were good friends, despite their different personalities. Cranmer was slow and cautious in introducing the Reformation into England; Cromwell's great energy paralleled his astounding political wisdom. It was he more than Cranmer who persuaded Henry VIII to issue an order that an English translation of the Bible be placed in every parish church.[26] When Cromwell was arrested in the council meeting, Cranmer interceded for him. He also wrote to the king, praising Cromwell for being an advisor who had loved the king and one whom he, Cranmer, had loved. He did allow for the fact that Cromwell may have been a traitor. When the vote in the House of Lords was taken condemning Cromwell, Cranmer let it be a unanimous one.[27]

Although Cranmer felt himself in danger in the triumph of the Roman Catholics over Cromwell, he was undisturbed. A more threatening event had occurred in 1539 when the king, fearful of a union of France, Spain, and the papacy against England, supported the passage of the famous Six Articles, which reversed England's drift in a Protestant direction. In reaffirming Roman Catholic teaching as the law of the land, the document included one article supporting an unmarried priesthood. Priests and their wives could be put to death for the crime of clergy marriage. Cranmer had respectfully objected to the king when the Six Articles were under discussion. The political pressure was such, however, that when the vote was taken in the House of Lords, Cranmer and other Protestant-minded bishops were forced to give open consent.[28]

Now Cranmer was forced to send his beloved wife, Margaret, back to Germany. He had been able to keep his marriage to her a closely guarded secret. As archbishop he had several residences; traveling between them, he used a chest with generous air holes to transport his wife. Apparently no one thought to paint "This Side Up" on both sides of the chest. Sometimes the porters left Margaret standing upside down—causing Roland Bainton to include her "among the minor martyrs of the Reformation"![29]

Yet if Cranmer had to dull his conscience in order to serve his king, there were times when he "spoke truth to power." He corrected a fourth of the king's revisions in a theological document the bishops planned to distribute.[30] Cranmer spoke in defense of allies like Anne

Boleyn and Thomas Cromwell. He marred his record, however, with the number of times he either presided at heresy trials or did nothing to save people with whom he sympathized from the fire. Because Henry VIII insisted that his subjects follow Roman Catholic theology and practice, Protestant dissenters grew in number. Some of these were Anabaptists, whom the archbishop saw as revolutionaries, and thus deserving of death. Some, like him, were opposed to the doctrine of transubstantiation and Real Presence. Much Protestant criticism fell on Cranmer for his helping to condemn these persons to death. In order to give the appearance of fairness he showed as much severity against Protestants as he did against Roman Catholics.[31]

For all that, Cranmer's relationship with Henry VIII was satisfying in many ways. Two events in 1543 assured the archbishop of the king's solid support. One April evening Henry invited Cranmer to his barge on the Thames River. During the intimate conversation Henry assured Cranmer that the Six Articles' prohibition against priestly marriage did not apply to him. Before the year was over Margaret Cranmer was secretly back in the archbishop's palace. Not long after that, Cranmer's conservative Roman Catholic enemies asked Henry to let Cranmer be tried for heresy in the council meeting. Henry agreed but summoned the archbishop, giving him a royal ring signifying the right of personal appeal to the king. The plot came to nothing.[32] When Henry died on January 27, 1547, it was Cranmer's hand that he held until his dying breath.

Archbishop Cranmer in the Reign of Edward VI

According to Henry's will, his son, Edward, by Jane Seymour, was to succeed him on the throne, with Mary and Elizabeth to follow in that order should all his children die childless. Sir John Cheke, an intimate friend of Cranmer's, had tutored Edward. The boy-king was an ardent Protestant. His uncle, Edward Seymour, the Duke of Somerset, who headed the privy council of advisors to the king, favored a Protestant policy.

As far as Rome was concerned, England now moved from schism to heresy. The Six Articles, known to Protestants as "the bloody whip with six strings," were repealed. Parliament made it law in 1547 that laypersons should receive the cup as well as the bread in the Lord's Supper. The leading Roman Catholic bishops were imprisoned because of their opposition. Cranmer had a hand in this.

The archbishop now could reform the church's liturgy. Even before Henry VIII's death, he had drawn up an English litany to be recited in all churches. The first complete service in English, it was a series of short prayers, prayer responses, and the Lord's Prayer. Because England was at war with Scotland in 1544, marching or processionals could also use this litany.

Cranmer continued in earnest. In 1547, while the mass was still being said in Latin, the epistle and Gospel lessons were chanted in English. The next year Parliament set forth "the Order of Communion" to appear in the Latin mass immediately following Communion by the priest. In the English language, it contained an exhortation and invitation to Communion, a confession of sin, absolution spoken by the priest, comfortable words of scripture, and the prayer of humble access. All these elements were later incorporated into the *Book of Common Prayer.*

On Pentecost 1549 the first *Book of Common Prayer,* Thomas Cranmer's "incomparable" liturgical achievement,[33] came into use. It reinterpreted the structure of the Roman mass in terms of the new Reformation theology and revealed Cranmer's broad acquaintance with recent liturgical developments in the Western church. Beyond the Latin mass, which served as a foundation and outline for his work, the archbishop drew upon some Roman Catholic reform-minded liturgies in Germany. He also used the work of the Spanish Cardinal Quinone, who had just completed his revision of the Roman breviary (the prayer book priests, monks, and nuns used daily) and the reformed liturgical work of Cologne's archbishop Hermann von Wied, who was later deposed for his Lutheranism. Cranmer wove all this material together into services of Holy Communion, Morning and Evening Prayer, and other liturgical pieces. His theological changes omitted many of the devotions to the Virgin Mary and the saints, the elevation of the host, and various prayers for the souls of the dead. Instead of any reference to the priest sacrificing Christ again on the altar, the consecration prayer referred to our Lord's "one oblation, once offered, a full, perfect, and sufficient sacrifice." The Lord's Supper was "a perpetuall [sic] memory of that his precious death."[34]

By 1548 Cranmer had converted to Zwingli's belief that the eucharistic bread and wine were but signs of the body and blood of Christ. Still he employed these words of administration: "The body of our Lord Jesus Christ which was given for thee, preserve thy soul and body unto everlasting life." The traditional priestly mass vestments were retained. In addition to its beautiful language, the new prayer book preserved the best of the traditional elements of mass, combining them with a greater reliance upon holy scripture. It has been called "a masterpiece of compromise, even of studied ambiguity."[35]

Cranmer did not expect the violent uprising the appearance of the 1549 prayer book caused. Reaction to the prayer book, mixed with rural unrest, had to be put down bloodily. One casualty was the duke of Somerset who, blamed for supporting the poor farmers, was executed for treason. His successor, the duke of Northumberland, gave Cranmer an even freer hand to promote the Reformation.

In 1552 Parliament adopted Cranmer's second *Book of Common*

Prayer, which was much more Protestant than its predecessor had been. Cranmer now eliminated the priestly mass vestments, removed altars from the chancel walls and made them Communion tables with legs. He inserted the Ten Commandments into the confession of sin and composed a special instructional statement that permitted people to kneel to receive the bread and wine on the condition they understood they were not kneeling to Christ's Real Presence in the elements. The new words of administration did not refer to the body and blood of Christ. In Zwinglian fashion communicants were instructed: "Take and eat this in remembrance that Christ died for thee; and feed on Him in thy heart by faith with thanksgiving."[36] Cranmer's 1552 prayer book was an artistic masterpiece. It did not attempt to be a revision of the Roman Catholic mass but was "the only effective attempt ever made to give liturgical expression to the doctrine of 'justification by faith alone.'"[37]

The prayer book of 1552 and the Forty-two Articles of Religion adopted in early 1553 never saw much usage in England. On July 6, 1553, Edward VI died of tubercular infection and, with his sister Mary's accession to the throne, England reverted to Roman Catholicism.

Archbishop Cranmer in the Reign of Queen Mary

Cranmer had reluctantly participated in an unsuccessful coup to prevent Henry VIII's daughter by Catherine of Aragon from assuming England's throne. When Mary was crowned queen, Protestant fears of recrimination and suppression were soon realized. Queen Mary restored the Roman mass to all England's parishes. She ordered the perpetrators of the coup to be beheaded or sent to the Tower of London. Mary released from prison the leading Roman Catholic bishops, Stephen Gardiner and Edmund Bonner, and restored them to leadership position. Replacing them in jail were the Protestant bishops Nicholas Ridley, Hugh Latimer, and John Hooper.

Cranmer knew what was in store for him. He sent Margaret and their two children to safety in Germany. When false rumors circulated that he offered to say the Roman mass before the queen and had reinstituted it at Canterbury, he wrote and distributed a statement declaring that the mass was the devil's invention and that the doctrine that existed in England under Edward VI was purer than any England had known for a thousand years![38] Mary's administration needed no further proof of the archbishop's heresy.

On September 13, 1553, Cranmer was arrested and sent to the Tower of London. Two months later Parliament tried and convicted him of treason. Despite a letter of apology Cranmer wrote to the queen, Mary condemned him to death.

The sentence was not immediately expedited, however. In March 1554 Cranmer, Ridley, and Latimer were transferred to an Oxford prison. On April 14 Cranmer stood alone for six hours while thirty-three Roman Catholic clergymen accused him. He maintained his Protestant beliefs. On October 16, 1555, from the roof of his prison he was forced to watch the burning of his friends Latimer and Ridley.

During his long confinement Cranmer sullied his career by writing a series of recantations of his Protestant beliefs and actions. Mary's government in London was delighted. A recantation by the arch-heretic would enhance her restoration of Catholicism to England. It would not save his life, however, as the "late archbishop" must have hoped. On February 14, 1556, Cranmer's degradation occurred. He was rudely stripped of the coarse, canvas archbishop's vestments he had been forced to wear. Two days later Cranmer signed another recantation subscribing without reservation to the doctrines and sacraments of the Roman Catholic church. Nonetheless, Mary wanted him dead for what he had done to her mother and to England.

On March 21, 1556, Cranmer went to the stake at Oxford. Because he was expected to recant his Protestant beliefs and actions publicly, he was allowed to speak in a ceremony held in the nearby church of St. Mary the Virgin. He read a beautiful prayer, said the Apostles' Creed, and then pulled from under his coat a prepared statement that included these lines:

> I now come to the great thing, which so much troubleth my conscience, more than any thing that ever I did or said in my whole life, and that is the setting abroad of writing contrary to the truth; which now here I renounce and refuse, as things written with my hand, contrary to the truth which I thought in my heart, and written for fear of death, and to save my life if it might be; and that is, all such bills and papers which I have written or signed with my hand since my degradation; wherein I have written many things untrue. And forasmuch as my hand offended, writing contrary to my heart, my hand shall first be punished therefore; for, may I come to the fire, it shall be first burned.[39]

As he was denouncing the pope as Christ's enemy and the Antichrist, Cranmer's executioners pulled him off the stage and hurried him to the fire. The archbishop kept his word. He held his right hand steadily in the fire, removing it only once to wipe his face. As the end came he committed himself to Christ, as did the dying Stephen. It was the greatest day of his life.

CRANMER'S UNDERSTANDING
OF THE CHRISTIAN FAITH

Thomas Cranmer did not write major theological works, as did his reformer counterparts on the continent. His heavy administrative responsibilities as archbishop and the political maneuvering he needed to do to promote the Reformation in England precluded any extensive publishing. However, Cranmer expressed himself in print upon two faith concerns.

The first of these, quite expectedly, was in the area of justification by grace through faith. In a book of *Homilies* (sermons) published in 1547, Cranmer declared himself on this subject. Writing with his usual clarity and excellent word choice, the archbishop declared that justification is by God's grace and not by our own human works: "But justification is the office of God only, and it is not a thing which we render unto him, but which we receive of him; not which we give to him, but which we take of him, by his free mercy, and by the only merits of his most dearly beloved Son, our only Redeemer, Savior, and Justifier, Jesus Christ."[40]

For Cranmer, humankind receives salvation only by "a true, lively, and unfeigned Christian faith."[41] This cannot be a mere creedal affirmation or even a casual assent to the gospel. Such would constitute a dead, idle faith. True faith manifests itself in fruits or results: "These be the fruits of the true faith: to do good, as much as lieth in us, to every man; and, above all things and in all things, to advance the glory of God, of whom only we have our sanctification, justification, salvation, and redemption."[42]

Salvation is by faith and not by works; faith is not vital and alive unless, having received the gift of God's saving grace, it also enables people to live beyond themselves to God's glory and their neighbors' good. Cranmer kept the balance between faith and good works.

Another noteworthy theological contribution of Cranmer's related to the Lord's Supper. In 1550 there appeared his *Defense of the True and Catholic Doctrine of the Sacrament of the Body and Blood of our Savior Christ.* In his treatise Cranmer attacked the doctrine of transubstantiation. Cranmer strongly criticized the Roman mass understood as a re-presentation of Christ's death on Calvary's cross, the veneration of the bread and wine of the Supper (Cranmer called it "idolatry"), and private masses which priests without a congregation said daily, receiving the bread and cup on behalf of absent lay worshipers. Little wonder that his criticisms aroused an attack by Bishop Gardiner, his chief Roman Catholic rival, who was in the Tower of London at the time.

The key issue, however, was the presence of Christ's human nature in the bread and wine. The Roman Catholic doctrine of transubstantiation insisted that the action of the Holy Spirit in the mass changed the bread and wine into the body and blood of Christ. The Lutheran teaching insisted that the bread and wine were not changed into the body and blood of Christ but that the latter, by the promise of the word, are really present in, with, and under the bread and wine. Cranmer by this time had been converted to the Zwinglian teaching. This held that the Apostles' Creed, in saying that our Lord had ascended into heaven to God's right hand and affirming that he will come again, clearly states that in his human form Christ cannot be present on the Communion table. Cranmer drew a distinction for both sacraments:

> And although Christ in his human nature substantially, really, corporeally, naturally, and sensibly, be present with his Father in heaven; yet sacramentally and spiritually he is here present in the water, bread, and wine, as in signs and sacraments; but he is indeed spiritually in the faithful Christian people, who

according to Christ's ordinance are baptized, or receive the holy communion, or unfeignedly believe in him.[43]

For Cranmer the bread and wine were not merely symbols but signs. They not only remind us of the incarnation and crucifixion of our Lord, but they "bring them before us"; they "exhibit" them in ways that we can understand.[44] Holding to his Zwinglian position, the archbishop claimed that Christ's spiritual, if not Christ's physical, presence was in the bread and wine. The Communion elements were much more than a bare reminder of Christ's life, death, and resurrection. In a unique way Christ spiritually met and nourished his followers at the table.

That too was an important point. Those who wish to receive anything at the table must be Christ's followers. They must be people who truly believe in the Lord. True eating and drinking at the Lord's table, said Cranmer, is accomplished as people believe with a constant and lively faith that Christ suffered on the cross for them and so "joins and incorporates himself to us" so that Christ is our head and we are Christ's members. Cranmer wanted to know what could give us more comfort than to eat and drink at this table "whereby Christ certifies us, that we are spiritually and truly fed and nourished by him, and that we dwell in him, and he in us."[45]

Cranmer again maintained a balance between the Holy Spirit's activity to guarantee Christ's presence in the bread and wine and our response of faith. Christ is not present because we think or believe so. Our faith does not "put" Christ in the bread and wine. The Lord who said "This is my body and blood" is spiritually present in the Supper in a unique way—and those who believe this rich promise and accept Christ's forgiving and nourishing grace are the ones who leave the Table filled and fulfilled.

Thomas Cranmer left contemporary believers at least two significant legacies that can enrich their Christian discipleship. The first is that he taught us how to pray. There seems to be little doubt that the *Book of Common Prayer* of 1549 and 1552 were largely Cranmer's creations. As a result he left behind the formal prayer models for much of Protestant worship.

Cranmer did something else. Raised in the Roman Catholic tradition and nurtured by his wide knowledge of the church fathers and the history of Christian worship, he valued the terse beauty of the collects the church had used for centuries in public worship. These brief prayers take their name from the Latin word *collecta*, because they collect or gather together the petitions of the people. Collects are often divided into four parts: an address to God; a relative clause often dealing with an attribute of God that explains the petition; the petition itself, which may be in agreement or in contrast to what is said about God's nature; and, finally, an expression of praise. Illustrative of this is the well-known Collect for Purity, which Cranmer lifted out of the Roman mass and placed at the beginning of his Holy Communion service: "Almighty God, unto whom all hearts are open, all desires known, and from whom no secrets are hid; cleanse the thoughts of our hearts by the inspiration of thy Holy Spirit, that we may perfectly love thee, and worthily magnify thy holy Name, through Christ our Lord. Amen."

Cranmer translated these collects and remolded many of them to agree with Protestant theology. The point is that he retained them and through the *Book of Common Prayer* has had a widespread influence on other English-speaking worship forms, particularly those of Presbyterian, United Church of Christ (Congregational), and Methodist traditions.

Of course, the differences Christians hold relative to worship and prayer are legitimate matters of taste. God surely hears prayer requests no matter by what formal or casual means each of us utters them. The collect form of prayer, however, can definitely enrich corporate worship. It offers a reverent alternative to unprepared prayers that call upon God without proper address or, forgetting to mention any of the divine attributes, parade forth a "laundry list" of petitions. The formal beauty of a collect lends dignity and depth to worship as something we do in God's house and in the special awareness of God's presence. It provides an escape from the unfortunate "Lord, we just want to praise you" informal prayers in wide use today, even in public prayer. Christians can find new and richer devotional expression through the use of the eloquent language in Cranmer's prayers.

The other insight Christians might glean from Thomas Cranmer's life story is that God can use submissive, hesitant, and inconsistent persons to accomplish significant things consistent with the divine purpose.

Thomas Cranmer had character flaws. Some have accused him of being more severe on fellow Protestants than on Roman Catholics—especially during Henry VIII's time. Some of his critics fault him for not having more zealously supported his friends, Anne Boleyn and Thomas Cromwell, when they were under Henry VIII's death sentence. Perhaps he was cowardly to be willing to sacrifice three radical Protestants if his Roman Catholic opponents would agree that three of their most vociferous representatives should also be burned in the "Smithfield fires" during King Henry's reign.[46]

We cannot avoid the fact that Cranmer, who perished at the stake with the Roman Catholic judgment of heresy upon him, had also been instrumental in sending people to the same fate. Nor can any easily claim that he died a hero's death. In order to save his life he issued six recantations of all he had written and accomplished as the Protestant archbishop of Canterbury. Only in his last moments did he repudiate these recantations and affirm his Protestantism by renouncing the pope just before he was led to the flames. He was a wavering hero, at best.

Yet there was a nobility about this man. In contrast to the ruthless Henry VIII, his benefactor, Cranmer was kind and merciful to his real enemies, Bishops Gardiner and Bonner. He interceded for Roman Catholics, Thomas More and John Fisher, whom Henry nonetheless beheaded. Ironically, it was Cranmer who, early on, persuaded Henry VIII not to send Mary to the Tower.[47] When the king was dissolving the monasteries and Cranmer could have realized considerable personal gain from the distribution of land and money, the archbishop took virtually nothing for himself. Cranmer also courageously opposed the pope and Roman Catholic doctrine, faltering in this only at the end of his life.

Beyond all this, there is something to be said for a gradual and cautious way of Reformation. If Cranmer sometimes appeared to be a servile churchman doing Henry VIII's dirty work without a twinge of conscience, we must remember that his genuine belief in royal supremacy over the church bound him to do the king's bidding. Additionally, he appears to have been equally astute as Henry VIII as a judge of character. He knew just how much he needed to give in to the king in order to wrest concessions from him. In fact, his submissiveness to Henry was the price he had to pay in order to remain in power during the reign of Edward VI. During those six years he had free reign to accomplish much for the Reformation. Whatever is said about Cranmer, we must acknowledge that he used his liturgical skills and the power of his office to give "his church a Bible, biblical preaching, a catechism, a Prayer Book and a confession of faith."[48] These, serving as the foundation upon which the Church of England would receive final formulation under Elizabeth I, were no meager accomplishments.

This account of Cranmer's life and leadership style does remind us of the role that resignation and compromise often play in achieving long-range goals. Perhaps there is strength hidden in Christian gentleness and quiet faith. Moreover, people learning to pray in their own language can be a powerful means of reforming the church. Cranmer's life recalls for us how the treasure of the gospel is faithfully handed on to successive generations, even though it is transmitted by God's use of some ordinary and limited "earthen vessels."

A PRAYER OF THOMAS CRANMER

Almighty and everlasting God, you are always more ready to hear than we to pray, and to give than we either desire or deserve: Pour upon us the abundance of your mercy, forgiving us those things of which our conscience is afraid, and giving us those good things for which we are not worthy to ask, except through the merits and mediation of Jesus Christ our Savior; who lives and reigns with you and the Holy Spirit, one God, for ever and ever. Amen.[49]

FOR PERSONAL OR GROUP REFLECTION

1. With what did you identify in Archbishop Cranmer's struggle for integrity? When have you found yourself in a position that made it difficult for you to do your work in good conscience?

2. Queen Mary and her half-sister, Queen Elizabeth, were quite different. Mary was staunch and unyielding in her faith; Elizabeth believed but was prone to compromise. How do you see these two

viewpoints at war in the church today? What kind of problems arise from each type of leadership? What different issues arise from these different approaches to faith?

3. In *Women of the Reformation in France and England,* Roland Bainton, after describing how some of the victims of martyrs' fires had earlier in their lives been responsible for the burning of others, drew the following conclusion: "The saints burn the saints. Those who believe strongly enough in an idea to die for it may be willing also to kill for it" (p. 207). How do you distinguish between victims and victimizers? What truth do you hear in Bainton's statement?

4. Is it good for Christians to be more like the willow than the oak? When is the strong defiance of the oak tree preferable to the gentle yielding of a willow? To which kind of discipleship are we Christians called?

5. In the setting of the English Reformation, laypersons and clergy had to be able to handle change. Try to imagine what you would have done had you lived in those turbulent times. How do you handle change in your fast-paced society? To what Christian resources do you personally turn when dealing with change?

6. Assess Thomas Cranmer's distinction between "a lively faith" (faith that expresses itself in doing good works) and "a dead faith" (faith that is merely passive without any active expression of good works). Consider periods in your life when you might best describe your Christian faith as "lively" or "dead"?

7. The medieval church did not want the holy scriptures in the hands of laypeople lest the latter make false and heretical interpretations of them. In what ways do you and other persons you know in the

church engage in serious study of the Bible? What place does regular Bible reading have in your faith formation?

8. What do you understand to be the benefits of Cranmer's efforts to create a common book of prayer for the church?

9. Cranmer is a person who, under great pressure, recanted something precious to him. When have you decided to take a radically different position on an important issue because of pressure from others? How did you feel afterward?

A Living Heritage

The Protestant Reformation of the sixteenth century was a monumental movement in world history. It shattered the unity of western Christendom and unleashed a new approach to life in theology, worship, government, work, education, and the arts. Dependent as it was on a growing nationalism in the countries of northern Europe, the Reformation enhanced a mood of independence as it broke entire peoples away from obedience to a central authority in Rome. In its protest against a number of medieval church regulations and acts of piety, it unwittingly contributed to a growing secularism in the world. Evaluating it from the vantage point of five hundred years prompts us to draw certain conclusions.

First, with all the advantage of hindsight, we can claim that it appeared to be inevitable. The many earlier enumerated protests against Roman domination of church and state in medieval Europe served as harbingers of a coming fragmentation of church unity and political peace. In fifteenth-century German lands especially, there was a growing hostility toward Rome. This resulted from the papacy's centuries-old domination of German emperors and its simultaneous acquisition of German money to spend in Italy in support of the arts and the church's desired opulence. Striking is Aleander's warning that as early as 1516 many Germans told him they were only waiting for "some fool" to open his mouth against

Rome.[1] The church's hierarchy little realized how out of touch it was with the common person of northern Europe.

Second, the Reformation, as the previous pages indicate, was often violent. Supported and opposed by political and military power, it had little chance of achieving its goals by strictly peaceful means. Many Roman Catholics and Protestants, with the exception of the Evangelical Anabaptists, were willing to use might to achieve and maintain what they thought was right. It is rather astounding that the great religious war in Europe that people feared in the sixteenth century was delayed about seventy years. The Thirty Years' War (1618–48), fought largely but not solely for religious reasons, devastated central Europe. Referred to as Europe's most destructive conflict until World War II, it caused horrible loss of life and property but altered the religious map of Europe very little. Sadly, Protestants and Catholics alike in both centuries considered the sword a legitimate weapon in support of their particular teaching of the cross.

Third, the Protestants failed in their effort at reforming the Roman Catholic church, although they were able to effect desired changes in the new denominations they created. They thereby illustrated how the church resists reformation and how division sometimes tends to become an easier solution than the artificial stretching of the bonds of inclusiveness in a united church. Left to themselves the Protestants were able to champion tenets like salvation by grace through faith; reliance upon biblical authority placed above church tradition; a simpler liturgy in the people's own language; an educated laity who were encouraged to read the holy scriptures; and a piety that stressed good works as a result, not the cause, of salvation. To varying degrees the legalism of the medieval church was laid aside. In a number of Protestant churches creeds that clergy and laity were expected to uphold summarized these gains.

Fourth, Protestantism's division into many churches and sects became the price it paid for its freedom from Rome. This was and continues to be Rome's major contention against Protestantism—that it had "rent the seamless robe of Christ." It is not encouraging to note that in the 1950s in the United States about two hundred and fifty Christian denominations existed. True, many of these could be classified into the major Lutheran, Presbyterian-Reformed, Anglican, Methodist, Baptist, and Anabaptist families. The disadvantages, however, that competitive rivalry and mutual denunciation create weaken the church's witness for Christ. Fortunately, a number of these churches have united in subsequent years.

Fifth, although it broke large segments of northern Europe's population away from the control of Rome, the Protestant Reformation inadvertently accomplished positive change in Roman Catholicism. Stung by the loss of so many million members and listening to voices of reform already being raised within its own household, the Roman church experienced its own reformation in the same century. This manifested itself in the election of far more serious-minded and pious popes than had been the case a century before. Strengthening this reform was the Jesuit order, established in 1540 by Ignatius Loyola (1491–1556). Loyola, a Spanish exsoldier, ran his society with military discipline. The Jesuit order founded excellent schools, established foreign missions, and enjoyed some success in winning Protestants in Germany and Poland back to the bosom of the Roman Catholic church. When the Roman Catholic bishops and theologians met at the Council of Trent intermittently between 1545 and 1563, they reaffirmed their church's doctrines, which the Protestants had attacked, and corrected some of the abuses the Protestants had deplored. Indeed, the Council of Trent transformed a beleaguered church into one much more able to withstand Protestant competition.

The Roman Catholic Reformation is a significant part of sixteenth-century church history.

Sixth, while Protestants were able to effect their cherished reform intentions in their own churches, the results were not pure gain. To be sure, they abolished what they considered to be superstitions that Roman Catholicism fostered. In so doing, however, some of them pushed the pendulum too far in an opposite and rationalistic direction. Those who veered off into a Unitarian emphasis lost the mystery connected with the doctrine of the Trinity and the insistence that our Lord is both human and divine. Those who denied their followers any assurance of Christ's presence in water, bread, and wine withdrew from them the comforts of sacramental grace. The tendency of some to stress only doctrinal purity accented the intellectual nature of the faith but deprived their adherents of the richness of the life of prayer and devotion. Not only did the Reformation shatter the unity of the church, but some loss of traditional spirituality occurred as well.

Seventh, the Protestant Reformation did create substantial reforms. These, of course, are best seen in its *solas:* "by grace alone, by faith alone, by Scripture alone." Luther initiated this; Zwingli continued it; Calvin magnified it. The latter's writings contain his abhorrence of "mixture."[2] He felt that the mass was a mixture of devout prayers of adoration with nonbiblical extravagance, that the "intoxicating" of humanity with unrealistic assurances of free will and human potential compromised God's glory. An accent upon a salvation partially obtained by the merits achieved by one's doing good works minimized Christ's all-sufficient sacrifice on the cross for our redemption. Calvin felt that prayers to the saints, and especially the Virgin Mary, eclipsed the high priesthood of Christ. Moreover, the authority for all this lay in the tradition of the church placed equally beside holy scriptures.[3]

The simplification of worship (particularly through the use of the vernacular language, the inspiration of stirring hymns, and the recovery of biblical preaching), the trust in Christ alone for salvation and intercession with God, and the stress on biblical authority were among Protestantism's considerable gains. It has been often and rightly contended that institutions are really the lengthened shadows of individuals. An observation of Lutheran, Presbyterian-Reformed and United Church of Christ, Mennonite, and Anglican (Episcopal) theology, worship patterns, and church life today yields discernible ties to the human founders of these various denominations.

Eighth, the Reformation never ended. It is with us still. Paul Tillich spoke of the "Protestant principle"—a "living, moving, restless power" that does not identify with any religious or political establishment (even Protestant churches) but constantly and prophetically critiques them all. This self-critical posture is by no means guaranteed, but it breaks forth whenever Holy Spirit-inspired clergy and laity submit to the judging and forgiving word contained in scripture.[4]

One of the major arguments between Protestants and Roman Catholics in the sixteenth century was that the former demanded reform of the church on a biblical basis while the latter conceded only to the necessity of reforms within the church, never wholesale reform of the church itself. They argued that the church was irreformable and its dogmas infallible.[5]

Interestingly, in the twentieth century, Roman Catholicism appears to have embraced the "Protestant principle" more than many Protestant denominations have. Beginning with Pope John XXIII and his desire to open the windows and let fresh air blow in the church and the changes that emerged from the Second Vatican Council of the 1960s, a noticeable shift in Roman Catholicism has occurred. Unlike the Protestant Reformation of five centuries ago, this has provided few theological revisions. What has occurred is change in liturgical practices, relaxation of certain piety restrictions, greater affirmation of biblical authority and preaching, and increased openness to the Protestant and Eastern Orthodox sections of Christianity.

Ninth, there are hopeful signs that some of the major differences existing between Protestants and Roman Catholics for five centuries may be eroding. Two events centered in twentieth-century Germany stand out among them. The first was the manner in which some German Roman Catholics and Protestants found unity in their negative reaction to the Nazi regime. One of Adolf Hitler's most outspoken critics was Cardinal Michael Faulhaber, archbishop of Munich. In 1935 he observed, "Catholic and Protestant are separated by many important matters of dogma, but there are great central convictions common to both and now subject to the sharpest attack. What we face today is a conflict not between two halves of Christianity, but between Christianity and the world."[6] A demonic totalitarian system requiring Christians in Germany to place their loyalty to God beneath their loyalty to the state enabled representatives of these two branches of Christianity to "find each other" in opposition to the common enemy.

Fifty years later a more benign opportunity invited Protestant and Roman Catholic cooperation. This was the five-hundredth anniversary of the birth of Martin Luther. Shortly before the November 10, 1983, observation, Lutheran and Roman Catholic theologians meeting in Milwaukee, Wisconsin, adopted a far-reaching agreement stating, "We can and do confess together that our hope for salvation rests entirely on God's merciful action in Christ."[7] In 1999, Vatican and Lutheran World Federation representatives came to a new appreciation of each other's positions. They declared, "Together we confess by grace alone, in faith in Christ's saving work and not because of any merit on our part, we are accepted by God and receive the Holy

Spirit, who renews our hearts while equipping and calling us to good works."[8] While not all differences have been removed, the thirty years of consultation have produced an amazing level of agreement.

Ecumenical discussions with Rome have also been undertaken by the Anglican, Presbyterian-Reformed, and Methodist world communions. As the globe seems to shrink and the separated branches of Christendom feel the need to draw together in the face of worldwide issues, the ecumenical movement, so long involving Protestant and Eastern Orthodox churches, may receive much fuller participation and support from Roman Catholicism.

A final observation is, perhaps, unnecessary but worth noting. Whatever judgments one wishes to make of the Protestant Reformation of the sixteenth century one would likely grant that, as a family fight, it was fraught with stirring events, compelling arguments, and colorful characters. It deserves four stars for providing an attention-holding drama of great consequence and for unleashing new energy into Western Christendom. True, it was a tragedy—as is any harsh separation in the body of Christ. For those who felt it was also a necessity, it achieved its purpose in winning for them a spirit of Christian freedom that enabled them under the authority of holy scripture and the direction of the Holy Spirit to live the life in Christ more faithfully and fruitfully. For this they, and we, raise voices in profound thanksgiving.

NOTES

PREFACE

1. Jaroslav Pelikan, *The Riddle of Roman Catholicism* (Nashville: Abingdon Press, 1959), 45f.

2. Robert McAfee Brown, *The Spirit of Protestantism* (New York: Oxford University Press, 1961), 40.

INTRODUCTION

1. E. Harris Harbison, *The Age of Reformation* (Ithaca, N.Y.: Cornell University Press, 1955), 16.

2. James M. Kittelson, *Luther the Reformer: The Story of the Man and His Career* (Minneapolis: Augsburg Publishing House, 1986), 133.

3. Ernest J. Schwiebert, *Luther and His Times: The Reformation from a New Perspective* (St. Louis: Concordia Publishing House, 1950), 361–79.

4. Harbison, *The Age of Reformation,* 12–13.

5. F. L. Carsten, "The Empire after the Thirty Years' War," in *The New Cambridge Modern History,* ed. F. L. Carsten (Cambridge: The University Press, 1961), 5:445.

6. H. F. M. Prescott, *Mary Tudor* (London: Eyre & Spottiswoode, 1953), 12.

7. Henry S. Lucas, *The Renaissance and the Reformation* (New York: Harper and Brothers Publishers, 1934), 146–47.

8. The author first learned this definition in a class in church history taught by Dr. Paul Eller in 1954 at the former Evangelical Theological Seminary in Naperville, Illinois.

9. John R. Hale, *Renaissance* (New York: Time Incorporated, 1965), 11.

10. James Mackinnon, *Luther and the Reformation* (London: Longmans, Green, and Company, 1925), 1:236.

11. William Stevenson, *The Story of the Reformation* (Richmond, Va.: John Knox Press, 1959), 24–25.

12. Hale, *Renaissance,* 91.

13. Mark U. Edwards Jr., *Printing, Propaganda, and Martin Luther* (Berkeley: University of California Press, 1994), 15.

14. Will Durant, *The Reformation,* Vol. 6 of *The Story of Civilization* (New York: Simon and Schuster, 1957), 160.

15. Cf. Philip S. Watson, *Let God Be God: An Interpretation of the Theology of Martin Luther* (London: The Epworth Press, 1947), 10.

CHAPTER 1

1. Carter Lindberg, *The European Reformations* (Oxford: Blackwell Publishers Ltd., 1996), 37.

2. Schwiebert, *Luther and His Times,* 128.

3. Kittelson, *Luther the Reformer,* 45–46.

4. D. Martin, *Luthers Werke* (Weimar Ausgabe) (Weimar: Hermann Böhlaus Nachfolger, 1910), 37:661; Schwiebert, *Luther and His Times,* 142.

5. Schwiebert, *Luther and His Times,* 146–47.

6. Richard Marius, *Martin Luther: The Christian between God and Death* (Cambridge, Mass.: The Belknap Press of Harvard University Press, 1999), 53; Kittelson, *Luther the Reformer,* 55.

7. Schwiebert, *Luther and His Times,* 150; Timothy George, *Theology of the Reformers* (Nashville: Broadman Press, 1988), 60.

8. David C. Steinmetz, *Luther and Staupitz: An Essay in the Intellectual Origins of the Protestant Reformation* (Durham, N.C.: Duke University Press, 1980), 3.

9. Heinrich Boehmer, *Road to Reformation: Martin Luther to the Year 1521,* trans. John W. Doberstein and Theodore G. Tappert (Philadelphia: Muhlenberg Press, 1946), 48.

10. Roland Bainton, *Here I Stand: A Life of Martin Luther* (Nashville: Abingdon Press, 1950), 51.

11. Alister E. McGrath, *Luther's Theology of the Cross: Martin Luther's Theological Breakthrough* (Oxford: Basil Blackwell, Ltd., 1985), 121.

12. Martin Luther, "Preface to the New Testament," in *Martin Luther: Selections from his Writings,* ed. John Dillenberger (Garden City, N.Y.: Doubleday & Company, Inc., 1961), 19.

13. E. Theodore Bachmann, ed., *Luther's Works* (Philadelphia: Muhlenberg Press, 1960), 35:236.

14. Kittelson, *Luther the Reformer,* 72–73.

15. A woodcut facsimile of this can be found in Bainton, *Here I Stand,* 31.

16. Schwiebert, *Luther and His Times,* 286.

17. Bainton, *Here I Stand,* 78.

18. Many Luther scholars accept the nailing-of-the-theses tradition. Others, like Scott Hendrix, admit that Luther only mentioned mailing them and that it was Philip Melanchthon who said Luther actually posted them. Scott H. Hendrix, *Luther and the Papacy: Stages in a Reformation Conflict* (Philadelphia: Fortress Press, 1981), 28.

19. Erik H. Erikson, *Young Man Luther: A Study in Psychoanalysis and History* (New York: W. W. Norton and Company, 1958), 228.

20. Harold J. Grimm, ed., *Luther's Works* (Philadelphia: Fortress Press, 1957), 31:55.

21. Schwiebert, *Luther and His Times,* 495.

22. Ibid., 499.

23. Ibid., 504–5.

24. Bainton, *Here I Stand,* 185.

25. John W. Doberstein, ed., *Luther's Works* (Philadelphia: Muhlenberg Press, 1959), 51:77–78.

26. Conrad Bergendoff, ed., *Luther's Works* (Philadelphia: Muhlenberg Press, 1958), 40:83.

27. Eric W. Gritsch, *Reformer without a Church: The Life and Thought of Thomas Münzer* (Philadelphia: Fortress Press, 1967), 144.

28. Robert C. Schultz, ed., *Luther's Works* (Philadelphia: Fortress Press, 1967), 46:50.

29. Bainton, *Here I Stand,* 286.

30. Ibid., 286–87.

31. Williston Walker, *A History of the Christian Church* (New York: Charles Scribner's Sons, 1959), 317.

32. See Theodore Tappert, ed. and trans., *Luther: Letters of Spiritual Counsel,* Vol. 28 of *The Library of Christian Classics* (Philadelphia: The Westminster Press, 1955), 50, 51, 76, 80, 166.

33. Roland Bainton, *Women of the Reformation in Germany and Italy* (Minneapolis: Augsburg Publishing House, 1971), 42.

34. Kittelson, *Luther the Reformer,* 300.

35. Martin Luther, *Three Treatises* (Philadelphia: Fortress Press, 1960), 9–111.

36. Ibid., 156.

37. Ibid., 163.

38. Ibid., 165.

39. Bergendoff, *Luther's Works,* 40:246.

40. Luther, *Three Treatises,* 277.

41. Ibid., 280.

42. Ibid., 309.

43. E. Gordon Rupp and Philip S. Watson, eds., *Luther and Erasmus: Free Will and Salvation,* Vol. 17 of *The Library of Christian Classics* (Philadelphia: The Westminster Press, 1969), 47.

44. Ibid., 96.

45. Ibid., 91.

46. Ibid., 106.

47. Ibid., 109.

48. Ibid., 38–40.

49. Ibid., 110–112.

50. Ibid., 232.

51. Ibid., 140.

52. Ibid., 141.

53. Ibid., 114.

54. Watson, *Let God Be God,* 33–38.

55. Doberstein, *Luther's Works,* 51:203–4.

56. Ibid., 95.

57. Jaroslav Pelikan, ed., *Luther's Works* (St. Louis: Concordia Publishing House, 1963), 26:38.

58. Watson, *Let God Be God,* 104.

59. Luther, *Three Treatises,* 286–288.

60. James Atkinson, ed., *Luther's Works* (Philadelphia: Fortress Press, 1966), 44:38.

61. Nehemiah Curdock, ed., *The Journal of the Rev. John Wesley, A. M.* (London: The Epworth Press, 1909), 475–76.

62. Dillenberger, *Martin Luther: Selections from His Writings,* 23–24.

63. Pelikan, *Luther's Works,* 12:322.

64. Tappert, *Luther: Letters of Spiritual Counsel,* 99–100.

65. Ibid., 34.

66. Doberstein, *Luther's Works,* 51:283.

67. Kittelson, *Luther the Reformer,* 210–12.

68. Clyde Manschreck, ed., *Prayers of the Reformers* (Philadelphia: Muhlenberg Press, 1958), 79.

CHAPTER 2

1. Jean Rilliet, *Zwingli: Third Man of the Reformation,* trans. Harold Knight (Philadelphia: The Westminster Press, 1959), 12.

2. G. W. Bromiley, ed., *Zwingli and Bullinger,* Vol. 23 of *The Library of Christian Classics* (Philadelphia: The Westminster Press, 1953), 13.

3. Jacques Courvoisier, *Zwingli: The Reformed Theologian* (Richmond, Va.: John Knox Press, 1963), 12.

4. G. R. Potter, ed., *Zwingli* (Cambridge: Cambridge University Press, 1976), 9.

5. John T. McNeill, *The History and Character of Calvinism* (New York: Oxford University Press, 1954), 21–22.

6. Rilliet, *Zwingli,* 27.

7. Oskar Farner, *Zwingli the Reformer: His Life and Work,* trans. D. G. Sear (New York: Philosophical Library, 1952), 27.

8. McNeill, *History and Character of Calvinism,* 26.

9. G. R. Potter, *Huldrych Zwingli* (New York: St. Martin's Press, 1977), 94.

10. Bromiley, *Zwingli and Bullinger,* 16–17.

11. Ulrich Gäbler, *Huldrych Zwingli: His Life and Work,* trans. Ruth C. L. Gritsch (Philadelphia: Fortress Press, 1986), 34.

12. McNeill, *History and Character of Calvinism,* 27.

13. Rilliet, *Zwingli,* 31–33.

14. Steven E. Ozment, *The Reformation in the Cities: The Appeal of Protestantism to Sixteenth-Century Germany and Switzerland* (New Haven, Conn.: Yale University Press, 1975), 59.

15. Lewis W. Spitz, *The Renaissance and Reformation Movements* (Chicago: Rand McNally and Company, 1971), 384.

16. McNeill, *History and Character of Calvinism,* 29.

17. Ibid., 30; Rilliet, *Zwingli,* 57–62.

18. Gottfried W. Locher, "The Change in the Understanding of Zwingli in Recent Research," *Church History* 34, no. 1 (March 1965): 19.

19. Fritz Büsser, "The Shepherd: Who Is the True Pastor?" *Christian History* 3, no. 1 (1984): 19.

20. Bromiley, *Zwingli and Bullinger,* 91.

21. Potter, *Zwingli,* 72.

22. Gäbler, *Huldrych Zwingli,* 53.

23. Farner, *Zwingli the Reformer,* 89.

24. Gäbler, *Huldrych Zwingli,* 56f.; McNeill, *History and Character of Calvinism,* 36.

25. Potter, *Huldrych Zwingli,* 21.

26. Ibid., 21–25.

27. Hans J. Hillerbrand, ed., *The Reformation: A Narrative History Related by Contemporary Observers and Participants* (New York: Harper and Row, 1964), 134–36.

28. Rilliet, *Zwingli,* 77–78.

29. Hillerbrand, *The Reformation,* 139–40.

30. Ibid., 142–43.

31. Fritz Büsser, "The Shepherd: Who Is the True Pastor?" 16–19, 35; Farner, *Zwingli the Reformer,* 56.

32. Bard Thompson, *Liturgies of the Western Church* (New York: The World Publishing Company, 1961), 141–56.

33. Farner, *Zwingli the Reformer,* 87.

34. McNeill, *History and Character of Calvinism,* 45; Gäbler, *Huldrych Zwingli,* 107–8.

35. William D. Maxwell, *An Outline of Christian Worship: Its Developments and Forms* (London: Oxford University Press, 1936), 86.

36. George, *Theology of the Reformers,* 129.

37. Potter, *Zwingli,* 221–24.

38. Farner, *Zwingli the Reformer,* 66.

39. McNeill, *History and Character of Calvinism,* 57.

40. Ibid., 64.

41. Farner, *Zwingli the Reformer,* 78; Potter, *Zwingli,* 260. A copy of the painting appears in Samuel Macauley Jackson, *Huldrych Zwingli: The Reformer of German Switzerland,* 1484–1531 (New York: G. P. Putnam's Sons, 1901), 286.

42. Potter, *Zwingli,* 257–62.

43. Bainton, *Women of the Reformation in Germany and Italy,* 55–76.

44. E. G. Rupp, "The Reformation in Zurich, Strassburg, and Geneva," in *The New Cambridge Modern History,* ed. G. R. Elton (Cambridge: Cambridge University Press, 1958), 2:107–12.

45. Potter, *Huldrych Zwingli,* 120.

46. Ibid., 107.

47. Potter, *Zwingli,* 348.

48. Potter, *Huldrych Zwingli,* 146.

49. Farner, *Zwingli the Reformer,* 133.

50. Potter, *Huldrych Zwingli,* 146.

51. McNeill, *History and Character of Calvinism,* 67.

52. Charles S. McCoy and J. Wayne Baker, *Fountainhead of Federalism: Heinrich Bullinger and the Covenantal Tradition* (Louisville, Ky.: Westminster/John Knox Press, 1991), 11–21; Wayne Baker, "Church, State, and Dissent: The Crisis of the Swiss Reformation, 1531–1536," *Church History* 57, no. 2 (June 1988): 135–52.

53. Walter Hollweg, *Heinrich Bullingers Hausbuch: Eine Untersuchung über die Anfänge der reformierten Predigtliteratur* (Giessen: Verlag der Buchhandlung des Erziehungsvereins Neukirchen Kreis Moers, 1956), 13.

54. Bromiley, *Zwingli and Bullinger,* 68.

55. Ibid., 72.

56. Ibid., 83.

57. Ibid., 80, 85.

58. Rilliet, *Zwingli,* 97–99.

59. Henry Emerson Fosdick, ed., *Great Voices of the Reformation: An Anthology* (New York: Random House, 1952), 162–63.

60. Ibid., 163.

61. Ibid., 163–65.

62. Rilliet, *Zwingli,* 38.

63. George, *Theology of the Reformers,* 122–26.

64. Fosdick, *Great Voices of the Reformation,* 165–69.

65. Bromiley, *Zwingli and Bullinger,* 138.

66. Ibid., 188.

67. Courvoisier, *Zwingli: The Reformed Theologian,* 28.

68. Bromiley, *Zwingli and Bullinger,* 63–66.

69. Ibid., 67.

70. Fosdick, *Great Voices of the Reformation,* 162.

71. Courvoisier, *Zwingli: The Reformed Theologian,* 41–42.

72. Bromiley, *Zwingli and Bullinger,* 270.

73. Courvoisier, *Zwingli: The Reformed Theologian,* 39.

74. Bromiley, *Zwingli and Bullinger,* 106.

75. Fosdick, *Great Voices of the Reformation,* 164.

76. Bromiley, *Zwingli and Bullinger,* 67.

77. Courvoisier, *Zwingli: The Reformed Theologian,* 29–33.

78. Bromiley, *Zwingli and Bullinger,* 84.

79. Ibid., 108.

80. Ibid., 113.

81. Ibid., 117.

82. Charles E. Hambrick-Stowe, "Ulrich Zwingli: Prophet of the Modern World," *The Christian Century* (4 April 1984): 338.

83. George, *Theology of the Reformers,* 161.

84. Ibid., 129.

CHAPTER 3

1. Georgia Harkness, *John Calvin: The Man and His Ethics* (New York: Henry Holt and Company, 1931), 258.

2. Spitz, *The Renaissance and Reformation Movements,* 412.

3. McNeill, *History and Character of Calvinism,* 227.

4. T. H. L. Parker, *Portrait of Calvin* (Philadelphia: The Westminster Press, 1954), 56–57.

5. William J. Bouwsma, *John Calvin: A Sixteenth Century Portrait* (Oxford: Oxford University Press, 1988), 5.

6. Ford Lewis Battles, ed. and trans., *The Piety of John Calvin: An Anthology Illustrative of the Spirituality of the Reformer* (Grand Rapids: Baker Book House, 1978), 31.

7. Hugh T. Kerr, ed., *By John Calvin: A Reflection Book: Introduction to the Writings of John Calvin* (New York: Association Press, 1960), 19.

8. John T. McNeill, ed., *Calvin: Institutes of the Christian Religion,* trans. Ford Lewis Battles, Vols. 20 and 21 of The Library of Christian Classics (Philadelphia: The Westminster Press, 1960), 20:7. Hereafter referred to as *Institutes.*

9. William Walker Rockwell, "Calvin and the Reformation," in *Three Addresses Delivered by Professors in Union Theological Seminary at a Service in Commemoration of the Four Hundredth Anniversary of the Birth of John Calvin* (New York: Union Theological Seminary, 1909), 10.

10. Jules Bonnet, ed., *Letters of John Calvin* (New York: Burt Franklin, 1972; original ed., 1858), 1:41.

11. William J. Petersen, "John Calvin's Search for the Right Wife," *Christian History* 5, (1986): 12–15.

12. Bonnet, *Letters of John Calvin,* 2:216.

13. McNeill, *History and Character of Calvinism,* 159.

14. Spitz, *The Renaissance and Reformation Movements,* 425.

15. Robert M. Kingdon, "The Control of Morals in Calvin's Geneva," in *The Social History of the Reformation,* ed. Lawrence P. Buck and Jonathan W. Zophy (Columbus, Ohio: Ohio State University Press, 1972), 9.

16. Robert M. Kingdon, *Church and Society in Reformation Europe* (London: Variorum Reprints, 1985), 52.

17. Benjamin W. Farley, ed., *John Calvin's Sermons on the Ten Commandments* (Grand Rapids: Baker Book House, 1980), 15.

18. McNeill, *History and Character of Calvinism,* 171.

19. Roland Bainton, *The Travail of Religious Liberty* (Philadelphia: The Westminster Press, 1951), 94.

20. T. H. L. Parker, *John Calvin: A Biography* (Philadelphia: The Westminster Press, 1975), 103.

21. *Institutes,* Book One, chap. I, sections 1–3.

22. Ibid., Book One, chap. VI, sections 2–3.

23. Ibid., Book One, chap. XIII, section 21.

24. Ibid., Book One, chap. XIII, section 7.

25. J. K. S. Reid, ed. and trans., *Calvin: Theological Treatises,* Vol. 22 of The Library of Christian Classics (Philadelphia: The Westminster Press, 1954), 129–30.

26. *Institutes,* Book One, chap. VII, section 4.

27. Ibid., Book One, chap. VI, section 2.

28. Ibid.

29. Ibid., Book One, chap. XVII, section 2.

30. Ibid., Book One, chap. XIV, section 22.

31. Ibid., Book One, chap. XV, section 4.

32. Ibid., Book One, chap. XIV, section 3.

33. Ibid., Book Two, chap. I, section 8.

34. Ibid., Book Two, chap. I, section 4.

35. John Calvin, "Instruction in Faith," in Fosdick, *Great Voices of the Reformation,* 218.

36. *Institutes,* Book One, chap. XV, section 8.

37. Ibid., Book Two, chap. III, section 5.

38. Francois Wendel, *Calvin: The Origins and Development of His Religious Thought,* trans. Philip Mairet (New York: Harper and Row Publishers, 1963), 186–87.

39. *Institutes,* Book Two, chap. I, section 8.

40. John Calvin, "The Proper Use of Scripture," in *The Mystery of Godliness and other Selected Sermons* (Grand Rapids: William B. Eerdmans Publishing Company, 1950), 135.

41. John Calvin, *Commentaries on the Book of the Prophet Jeremiah and Lamentations,* ed. Rev. John Owen (Grand Rapids: Baker Book House, reprint 1979), 3:141–42.

42. Dirk Jellema, "God's 'Baby-Talk': Calvin and the 'Errors' in the Bible," *The Reformed Journal* (April 1980): 25–27.

43. *Institutes,* Book Two, chap. VI, section 4.

44. Ibid., Book Three, chap. XXI, section 5.

45. Wendel, *Calvin,* 266–67.

46. David W. and Thomas F. Torrance, eds., *Calvin's Commentaries: The Gospel According to St. John 1–10,* trans. T. H. L. Parker (Grand Rapids: William B. Eerdmans Publishing Company, 1959), 75.

47. Wilhelm Niesel, *The Theology of John Calvin,* trans. Harold Knight (Philadelphia: The Westminster Press, 1956), 164.

48. *Institutes,* Book Three, chap. II, section 7.

49. Ibid., Book Three, chap. XXII, section 10.

50. Calvin, "The Doctrine of Election" in *The Mystery of Godliness,* 43.

51. David W. and Thomas F. Torrance, eds., *Calvin's Commentaries: The Epistle of Paul the Apostle to the Galatians, Ephesians, Philippians, and Colossians* (Edinburgh: Oliver and Boyd, 1965), 125.

52. *Institutes,* Book Two, chap. VII, section 12.

53. Farley, *John Calvin's Sermons on the Ten Commandments,* 282–283.

54. *Institutes,* Book Four, chap. I, section 9.

55. Ibid., Book Four, chap. I, section 4.

56. Ibid., Book Four, chap. I, section 8.

57. Ibid., Book Four, chap. XIV, section 6.

58. Ibid., Book Four, chap. XIV, section 1–7.

59. Ibid., Book Four, chap. XVII, section 18.

60. Ibid., Book Four, chap. XVII, section 3.

61. *Westminster Shorter Catechism* (The Constitution of the Presbyterian Church [U.S.A.] Part I, The Book of Confessions (New York and Atlanta: Office of the General Assembly, 1983), 7.001.

62. John C. Olin, ed., *A Reformation Debate: Sadoleto's Letter to the Genevans and Calvin's Reply* (New York: Harper and Row Publishers, 1966), 58.

63. *Institutes,* Book One, chap. I, section 1.

64. Ibid., Book Three, chap. III, section 5.

65. Ibid., Book Three, chap. II, section 24.

66. John H. Leith, *John Calvin's Doctrine of the Christian Life* (Louisville, Ky.: Westminster/John Knox Press, 1989), 40.

67. *Institutes,* Book Two, chap. II, section 17.

68. Thomas F. Torrance, ed., *Tracts and Treatises on the Reformation of the Church,* trans. Henry Beveridge (Grand Rapids: William B. Eerdmans Publishing Company, 1958) 1:134.

69. Ibid., 159–60.

70. *Institutes,* Book Two, chap. III, section 8.

71. Ibid., Book Three, chap. VII, section 2.

72. Ibid., Book Three, chap. XX, section 14.

73. Battles, *The Piety of John Calvin,* 34.

74. David W. and Thomas F. Torrance, eds., *Calvin's Commentaries: The Epistle of Paul the Apostle to the Hebrews and the Epistles of Peter* (Edinburgh, London: Oliver and Boyd, 1963), 211.

75. *Institutes,* Book Three, chap. VII, section 1.

76. Ibid., Book Four, chap. XX, sections 30–31.

77. Lester De Koster, "Keep the Church Out of—What?" *The Christian Century* (29 March 1967): 404.

78. Fosdick, *Great Voices of the Reformation,* 201.

79. Daniel Buscarlet, *International Monument of Reformation* (Geneva, Switzerland: Editions L'Eau Vive, 1959), 3–10.

80. Manschreck, *Prayers of the Reformers,* 79.

CHAPTER 4

1. Hillerbrand, *The Reformation,* 242–45.

2. Mark H. Tuttle, ed., "The Radical Reformation: The Anabaptists," *Christian History* 4, no. 1 (1985): 6.

3. Ibid., 27.

4. George Hunston Williams, *The Radical Reformation,* 3rd ed. (Kirksville, Mo.: Sixteenth Century Journal Publishers, Inc., 1992), 1303ff. See also Roland Bainton, *The Reformation of the Sixteenth Century* (Boston: The Beacon Press, 1952), 95.

5. Franklin H. Littell, *The Anabaptist View of the Church: A Study in the Origins of Sectarian Protestantism,* 2nd ed. (Boston: Starr King Press, 1958), 46ff.

6. Hans J. Hillerbrand, "Radicalism in the Early Reformation," in *Radical Tendencies in the Reformation: Divergent Perspectives,* ed. Hans J. Hillerbrand (Kirksville, Mo.: Sixteenth Century Journal Publishers, Inc., 1988), 36.

7. Balthasar Hubmaier, "On Free Will," in *Spiritual and Anabaptist Writers,* ed. George Huntston Williams, Vol. 25 of *The Library of Christian Classics* (Philadelphia: The Westminster Press, 1957), 129.

8. Littell, *The Anabaptist View of the Church,* 46.

9. John C. Wenger, ed., *The Complete Writings of Menno Simons* (Scottdale, Penn.: Mennonite Publishing House, 1956), 189, 233, 310, 1052–1054. See also Hans-Jürgen Goertz, *The Anabaptists,* trans. Trevor Johnson (London and New York: Routledge, 1996), 73.

10. Ibid., 274.

11. Ibid., 272.

12. Ibid., 264–65.

13. Bainton, *The Reformation of the Sixteenth Century,* 99.

14. Fosdick, *Great Voices of the Reformation,* 288.

15. Williams, *Spiritual and Anabaptist Writers,* 246–47.

16. George, *Theology of the Reformers,* 297.

17. Ibid.

18. N. Van Der Sijpp, "The Early Dutch Anabaptists," in *The Recovery of the Anabaptist Vision,* ed. Guy F. Hershberger (Scottdale, Penn.: Herald Press, 1957), 80, 33f.

19. George, *Theology of the Reformers,* 281.

20. Williams, *The Radical Reformation,* 494.

21. Ibid., 493.

22. Willem Balke, *Calvin and the Anabaptist Radicals,* trans. William J. Heynen (Grand Rapids: William B. Eerdmans Publishing Company, 1981), 204–5.

23. "The Church of God" in Williams, *Spiritual and Anabaptist Writers,* 251.

24. Fosdick, *Great Voices of the Reformation,* 290–94.

25. "Letters to Thomas Münzer" in Williams, *Spiritual and Anabaptist Writers,* 78–79.

26. Williams, *The Radical Reformation,* 1240; Walter Klaasen, *Anabaptism: Neither Catholic Nor Protestant* (Waterloo, Ont.: Conrad Press, 1973), 21.

27. Alvin J. Beachy, *The Concept of Grace in the Radical Reformation* (Nieuwkoop: B. DeGraff, 1977), 127–28.

28. Littell, *The Anabaptist View of the Church,* 112.

29. Hans Hut, "On the Mystery of Baptism," in *Early Anabaptist Spirituality,* ed. Daniel Liechty (Mahwah, N.J.: Paulist Press, 1994), 69.

30. Littell, *The Anabaptist View of the Church,* 112.

31. George Hunston Williams effectively classified these various groups in the introduction to his *Spiritual and Anabaptist Writers,* 19–38. See also his *The Polish Brethren: Documentation of the History and Thought of Unitarianism in the Polish-Lithuanian Commonwealth and in the Diaspora,* 1601–1685 (Missoula, Mont.: Scholars Press, 1980), 47.

32. The Hutterites and the Amish are excluded from commentary here only because of their smaller size. The followers of Jacob Hutter understood the Christian life largely in terms of *Gemeinschaft* (community) in which all things

were owned in common. Their excellent farm settlements are to be found today in Canada and in North and South Dakota. The Amish, whose large farms, simple lifestyle, and horse-drawn transportation make them stand out in such states as Pennsylvania, Ohio, Indiana, and Illinois especially, emerged in Switzerland in 1693 when their leader, Jacob Ammann (1661?–1730) led an unsuccessful reform movement among the Swiss Brethren.

33. H. Wayne Pipkin and John H. Yoder, eds., *Balthasar Hubmaier: Theologian of Anabaptism* (Scottdale, Penn., and Kitchener, Ont.: Herald Press, 1989), 81–82.

34. Williams, *Spiritual and Anabaptist Writers,* 29.

35. Goertz, *The Anabaptists,* 105–6.

36. Ernest A. Payne, "The Anabaptists," in Elton, *The New Cambridge Modern History,* 2:127.

37. George, *Theology of the Reformers,* 257.

38. Harold S. Bender, "A Brief Biography of Menno Simons" in Wenger, *The Complete Writings of Menno Simons,* 4.

39. "A Meditation on the Twenty-fifth Psalm" in Liechty, *Early Anabaptist Spirituality,* 262.

40. Wenger, *Complete Works of Menno Simons,* 668.

41. Ibid., 671.

42. John Horsch, *Menno Simons: His Life, Labors, and Teaching* (Scottdale, Penn.: published by the author, 1916), 179.

43. Bender, *A Brief Biography of Menno Simons,* 16–19.

44. George, *Theology of the Reformers,* 263.

45. Williams, *The Radical Reformation,* 738, 747.

46. Hans J. Hillerbrand, "Menno Simons—Sixteenth Century Reformer," in *Church History* 31, no. 4 (December 1962): 387–88.

47. Bender, *A Brief Biography of Menno Simons,* 28.

48. William R. Estep, *The Anabaptist Story: An Introduction to Sixteenth Century Anabaptism,* 3rd edition (Grand Rapids: William B. Eerdmans Publishing Company, 1996), 170–74.

49. Interestingly, Menno's position on the celestial flesh of Christ was not acceptable to the Swiss Mennonites. Although it influenced the Dutch and North German Mennonites somewhat, "it never found its way into any authoritative creed or confession of the Mennonite Church."—Bender, *A Brief Biography of Menno Simons,* 14.

50. Wenger, *Complete Works of Menno Simons,* 96–97.

51. Ibid., 739–42.

52. Ibid., 734.

53. Ibid., 774.

54. Hillerbrand, "Menno Simons—Sixteenth Century Reformer," 396–97.

55. Wenger, *Complete Works of Menno Simons,* 601.

56. Ibid., 614.

57. Ibid., 618–19.

58. Ibid., 93.

59. Bender, *A Brief Biography of Menno Simons,* 16.

60. Estep, *The Anabaptist Story,* 174.

61. Wenger, *Complete Works of Menno Simons,* 1069.

CHAPTER 5

1. Bainton, *The Reformation of the Sixteenth Century,* 208.

2. Sir Maurice Powicke, *The Reformation in England* (London: Oxford University Press, 1941), 1.

3. Harbison, *The Age of Reformation,* 69.

4. A. G. Dickens, *The English Reformation* (New York: Schocken Books, 1964), 57.

5. The six wives of Henry VIII were Catherine of Aragon (1509–32), mother of Mary I; Anne Boleyn (1533–36), mother of Elizabeth I; Jane Seymour (1536–37), mother of Edward VI; Ann of Cleves (1540); Catherine Howard (1540–42); Catherine Parr (1543–47). The easiest way to remember the fate of Henry's wives is to make use of the couplet: "Divorced, beheaded, died, divorced, beheaded, survived."

6. Roland Bainton, *Women of the Reformation in France and England* (Minneapolis: Augsburg Publishing House, 1973), 231.

7. Dr. Paul Eller, class lecture, Evangelical Theological Seminary, Naperville, Illinois (Fall Quarter, 1954).

8. Tony Lane, "A Man for All People: Introducing William Tyndale," *Christian History* 6, no. 4 (1987): 6–7.

9. Carl R. Trueman, *Luther's Legacy: Salvation and the English Reformers* (Oxford: Clarendon Press, 1994), 12.

10. John R. H. Moorman, *A History of the Church in England* (New York: Morehouse-Barlow Company, 1959), 172.

11. F. E. Hutchinson, *Cranmer and the English Reformation* (New York: The Macmillan Company, 1951), 16.

12. Donald Smeeton, "The Bible Translator Who Shook Henry VIII," *Christian History* 6, no. 4 (1987): 18.

13. Lane, *A Man for All People,* 8.

14. Dickens, *The English Reformation,* 131–32. Rogers used the pseudonym "Thomas Matthew." His work was called the "Matthew Bible."

15. "Did You Know?" *Christian History* 6, no. 4 (1987): 4.

16. Theodore Maynard, *The Life of Thomas Cranmer* (Chicago: Henry Regnery Company, 1956), 13.

17. Jasper Ridley, *Thomas Cránmer* (Oxford: Clarendon Press, 1962), 16.

18. Ibid., 20–23.

19. Maynard, *Life of Thomas Cranmer,* 35–43.

20. Ridley, *Thomas Cranmer,* 39–54.

21. Ibid., 54–57.

22. Philip Hughes, *The Reformation in England,* 5th revised edition in three volumes (New York: Macmillan, 1963), 1:243.

23. Peter Newman Brooks, *Cranmer in Context: Documents from the English Reformation* (Minneapolis: Fortress Press, 1989), 29.

24. Ridley, *Thomas Cranmer,* 257.

25. Ibid., 96.

26. Ibid., 127.

27. Ibid., 201–4.

28. Ibid., 186–91.

29. Bainton, *The Reformation of the Sixteenth Century,* 198.

30. Ridley, *Thomas Cranmer,* 122–24.

31. Ibid., 231.

32. Ibid., 235–39.

33. Brooks, *Cranmer in Context,* 52.

34. Thompson, *Liturgies of the Western Church,* 235.

35. Dickens, *The English Reformation,* 219.

36. It was in the Elizabethan Settlement of 1559 that the words of administration of the 1549 prayer book were joined together in sequence with those of 1552. They are still the words spoken to communicants at Episcopal and Anglican altars today.

37. Dom Gregory Dix, *The Shape of the Liturgy* (Westminster: Dacre Press, 1945, reprint 1954), 672.

38. Ridley, *Thomas Cranmer,* 351.

39. Brooks, *Cranmer in Context,* 116. The text from which Cranmer had read was dropped near the fire and fortunately preserved for posterity.

40. Thomas Cranmer, "Certain Sermons, or Homilies" in *English Reformers,* ed. T. H. L. Parker, Vol. 26 of *The Library of Christian Classics* (Philadelphia: The Westminster Press, 1956), 267.

41. Ibid., 273.

42. Ibid., 271.

43. Quoted in *Writings of the Rev. Dr. Thomas Cranmer* (London: The Religious Tract Society, n.d.), 239.

44. G. W. Bromiley, *Thomas Cranmer, Theologian* (New York: Oxford University Press, 1956), 74.

45. *Writings of the Rev. Dr. Thomas Cranmer,* 235.

46. Ridley, *Thomas Cranmer,* 207.

47. Ibid., 75–76.

48. Bromiley, *Thomas Cranmer, Theologian,* 9.

49. Proper 22, the Sunday closest to October 5, *Book of Common Prayer* and *Administration of the Sacraments and Other Rites and Ceremonies of the Church* (The Church Hymnal Corporation and the Seabury Press, 1979), 234.

CONCLUSION

1. Durant, *The Reformation,* 332.

2. Bouwsma, *John Calvin,* 34f.

3. A summation of this can be found in Torrance, *John Calvin: Tracts and Treatises on the Reformation of the Church,* 1:134–35.

4. Paul Tillich, *The Protestant Era,* trans. James Luther Adams (Chicago: The University of Chicago Press, 1948), 162–63.

5. Brown, *The Spirit of Protestantism,* 45.

6. Ruth Rouse and Stephen Neill, eds., *A History of the Ecumenical Movement* (Philadelphia: The Westminster Press, 1954), 586.

7. "Retracing the Reformation," *Time* (3 October 1983): 74.

8. "Agreeing on Justification," *The Christian Century* (June 30–July 7, 1999): 669–70.